John M. Knapp

The Universities and the Social Problem

An Account of the University Settlements in East London

John M. Knapp

The Universities and the Social Problem
An Account of the University Settlements in East London

ISBN/EAN: 9783743384118

Manufactured in Europe, USA, Canada, Australia, Japa

Cover: Foto ©Suzi / pixelio.de

Manufactured and distributed by brebook publishing software (www.brebook.com)

John M. Knapp

The Universities and the Social Problem

THE UNIVERSITIES

AND THE SOCIAL PROBLEM

An Account of the
University Settlements in East London

EDITED BY JOHN M. KNAPP

THE OXFORD HOUSE, BETHNAL GREEN

RIVINGTON, PERCIVAL & CO.

KING STREET, COVENT GARDEN

LONDON

1895

PREFACE.

"WHAT do you do when you go down to the East End ?" is a question which the resident in a Settlement is continually being asked by his friends "up West," or in the country. The object of this volume is to give some account of the work which has already been accomplished, and which it is hoped to accomplish, towards the solution of the ever-present Social Problem by means of "Settlements," at which the young men—and young women—of the great Universities and Schools are enabled to live in the heart of the East End, and to endeavour in various ways to brighten the lives of their less fortunate fellow-creatures. Papers are written by the Heads of Oxford House (the Church Settlement), Toynbee Hall, and Mansfield House (the Nonconformist Settlement) ; the methods and aims of the two Bethnal Green Settlements for Ladies are discussed by duly qualified residents ; the College and School Missions are exemplified by papers from the Magdalen College Mission, and the new Repton Club for Rough Boys ; and various other East End topics are treated by members of the different Settlements.

I have to express my best thanks to Sir John Gorst for allowing me to make use of his Glasgow Rectorial Address, which is printed as an introduction to this volume ; and also to signify my gratitude to the various contributors thereto, and particularly to those of them who have been kind enough to help me with suggestions and criticism.

It has been, of course, impossible to include in a book of this size all the subjects and all the writers whom I should have liked to include.   Enough will probably be found in the following pages to show the reader that there is great diversity of opinion and practice among those even who are working on fairly similar lines towards the solution of social problems in the East End. I need hardly say that no one writer is to be held as being necessarily in agreement with all that his fellow contributors may think or say.

If the perusal of this little book should lead to further interest being taken in, and further support being given to, our University Settlements, it will not have been put together in vain.

J. M. K.

CONTENTS

" SETTLEMENTS "
IN ENGLAND AND AMERICA

BY THE

RIGHT HON. SIR JOHN GORST, M.P.

B

"SETTLEMENTS"
IN ENGLAND AND AMERICA.[1]

IN the course of this book it is proposed to call attention to the obligations which the classes who possess culture and leisure have towards those who are less richly endowed ; to the necessity of applying knowledge and research to solve the social problems of the day; and to the practical efforts made in this direction by University Settlements in the poorest quarters of our great cities.

The congregation of the wage-earning classes in districts of their own is a product of modern civilization. In olden times, whatever the distinction of classes, rich and poor lived side by side. The master constantly beheld the homes of his men, and was a witness of the events of their social life. In affliction the men could appeal to the sympathy and help which human beings will usually accord to present visible distress. The railways have altered all this. Both parties have left the spot on which their livelihood depends : the rich, for luxurious homes far removed from the sight of misery and from contact

[1] The substance of an address to the University of Glasgow, delivered on November 2, 1894.

with the poor ; the poor, for districts inhabited almost
exclusively by those whose means are scanty, and in
which very few persons of culture or leisure are to be
found.   This freshly opened gulf between rich and
poor has produced evil results on the character of
both classes, and is a disorder of the body politic for
which a remedy is urgently needed.   The case would
be bad enough if all the people who live in such a
neighbourhood were able to earn their living, but the
poor quarters of the great cities become the home of
the unemployed of all the surrounding country.   The
same railways which have carried off the rich, bring
in the destitute to take their chance of sharing the
casual jobs and the spasmodic charities of a great
city.   Society would be glad, for the sake of its own
peace of mind, to believe that the workers who
cannot earn a living are composed, as is sometimes
alleged, entirely of criminals and loafers.   But this
is not the case.   The criminals and loafers—of whom
many have been made such by the social circumstances
in which they have been placed—form a small percentage only of the class of miserably poor in great
cities.   The great majority, who are both able and
willing to work, are composed of two classes—(1)
those, like dock labourers, whose work is irregular
and intermittent, and who are unable on an average
throughout the year to earn a living wage ; and (2)
the workers of the sweated industries, who cannot by
unremitting toil obtain money enough to defray the
cost of food, clothes, and lodging.   Even the families
of workers earning fair and regular wages live in a
state of precarious prosperity.   Sickness, accident,

or death may in a moment deprive them of their support, and reduce them into the ranks of the poor.

Whether the proportion of those who cannot gain a living is in this or any other country on the increase seems a question which society has not at present the means of answering. But modern civilization has certainly had the effect of concentrating the destitute classes, and of making their existence thereby more conspicuous and more dangerous. In London and many of our British cities, in the older cities of America and Australia, in many of the European capitals, they already form a substantial part of the population, and possess even now, though they are still ignorant of their full power, great political importance.

The study of this alarming phenomenon of modern society is one to which the highest intellect, the most earnest research, and the most unwearied industry may not unworthily be consecrated. Even if the evil goes no further, the fact that a large portion of mankind, neither idle nor vicious, spend their lives in an unsuccessful struggle to provide themselves and their families with the barest necessaries is a reproach to our Christianity and civilization. While such a state of things is unremedied, it is only by going away, shutting their eyes and ears to facts, and wrapping themselves up in class egotism, that the leisured can enjoy the culture and refinement to which they have attained. But the evil may be on the increase. Almost every winter in London there is a panic lest the condition of the poor should become intolerable. The richer classes awake for a moment from their apathy, and salve their consciences by a subscription of money, which, if it occasionally relieves acute distress, makes things in the end far worse than at the first. The annual alarm may some day prove a reality, and the destitute classes may swell to such proportion as to render the continuance of our existent social system impossible. If the wisdom of the more highly educated cannot find a remedy, the desperate sufferers may be driven to try one of their own. They could do this without any lawless outbreak, leading to their suppression by armed force, by their lawful power at the polls. Their remedy might be an entirely wrong one, and might in the end aggravate the disease, but it is not impossible that many of the best results of our social progress might perish in the experiment. The instinct of self-preservation should, therefore, make society grateful to anybody who will spend his life in gaining the confidence of the masses and guiding their ideas into channels in which the common good of all is the prevailing influence.

The motives which prompt a man or woman of refinement and culture to settle in a neighbourhood in which both are conspicuously absent are various, and are possibly not very exactly analyzed by some of the settlers themselves. There is, in the first place, the desire for activity natural to every young and healthy intellect. Some, at least, of the men and women trained at our universities do not find in the professions or in the business of money-making an adequate outlet for their mental faculties. The consciousness of possessing a talent stirs them to make use of it. They do not wish to lay it up in a napkin, but to trade with it. They find in work amongst the poor an outlet for superfluous energy, and a satisfaction of intellectual craving. Then, there is the missionary spirit, which prompts the possessor of any kind of knowledge to spread it amongst his fellow-men. It was this which gave rise to the University Extension movement; and the University Settlement, in which the former movement finds a congenial centre, is its natural and logical outcome. It is true that the settlements were founded for social, not for educational objects, but they have proved to be most effective instruments for the latter as well as the former. There is, again, that irresistible propensity which some persons have to renounce the accidental advantages of birth and fortune, and to go down into the common arena to join in the struggle for existence with their fellow-men. The head of one of the most illustrious families of the nobility of Scotland spent the best years of his life as a seaman before the mast. Even persons who show no outward sign in their lives, shut up in their hearts a sense of mortification at their uselessness. They long to have something to do; they envy the lot of the active, useful members of society. Miss Addams, of Chicago, who recognizes this desire to share the "race life" as one of the principal causes which induce women in particular to settle amongst the poor, and take part in their troubles, thinks it has its origin in the struggle for existence of primeval man, and is an instinct inherited from our far-off ancestors. But whatever the origin may be, and whether the sentiment be praiseworthy or not, there is no doubt of the existence of such a propensity, and that the life in a University Settlement gives it a legitimate and useful direction.

There is also among the young a general desire for equality, which finds its satisfaction in fraternizing with the poor. Children are born with no sense of the distinctions of rank and fortune. They will fondle a negro or a Hottentot as readily as one of their own colour ; they will share their toys with poor neighbours who have none. The lesson of class differences has to be taught artificially and sometimes painfully. Some never learn it, but remain sturdy levellers throughout life. Some conform to the rules of society in their outward conduct, when cherishing in their inmost souls a feeling of revolt against the injustice and dissimulation which they have to practise. Mere political equality does not satisfy this craving. It may coexist with the grossest social injustice. In the United States negroes have equal political rights with the white population, but live in social ostracism. Nor is it much good that the Christian religion inculcates the social equality of all men as a doctrine, for Christian society will not admit it, even as a theory in social life. What people in society ever dream of seeking out as guests the poor, the maimed, the lame, and the blind, or conceive that it is their duty to use their social position for any other purpose than the promotion of their own amusement or their own social advancement ? Even in public official entertainments, paid for practically by public money, there is a conspicuous absence of the members of those classes whose votes place the giver of the entertainment in power, and whose money contributes the greater portion of its cost.

I do not pretend to give a complete catalogue of the motives by which University Settlements are recruited, but there is one more that I must refer to, more important than any that I have yet mentioned. It is the revival, as a real force for the guidance of human life, of the doctrines taught by Jesus Christ and practised by the Christians of the first century. It is the recognition of the image of God in the most fallen and debased of the human race, and the conviction that the only life worth living is one in which the talents and capacities of the individual are spent in the service of mankind. To young men and women animated by such a belief the conditions of modern society are intolerable. The charity which consists in subscriptions, bazaars, and public meetings cannot satisfy their desires. They long to come into personal contact with human suffering, to bind up the wounds with their own hands, to pour in oil and wine from their own stores, to give up their own beast and go on foot themselves, and to welcome the afflicted to their own society and their own abode. Gifts of money cannot cure the misery of the poor, it is fortunate if they do not aggravate them ; duty to your neighbour cannot be done by deputy ; the life of devotion to the good of the human race at large, which is the religion of Jesus Christ, demands personal service. I should be sorry to suggest that there is no other outlet for such a sentiment than residence in a University Settlement, or even life amongst the poor. The noble deeds recorded in history prove that the Spirit of Christ can manifest itself in many ways. But the University Settlement affords a very obvious and natural outlet for such feelings, and a large proportion of the residents in all the settlements are animated, whether consciously or unconsciously, by Christian love of the human race.

Having now dealt with the subjective motives which induce the formation of settlements, let us consider next their aims and practical proceedings.

All settlements, both in England and America, seem to be begun upon one uniform principle. The first object, to which every other is subsidiary, is to make friends with the neighbourhood—to become part of its common life ; to associate with the people on equal terms, without either patronage on the one side or subserviency on the other ; to share in the joys and sorrows, the occupations and amusements of the people ; to bring them to regard the members of the settlement as their friends. The name of the New York settlement is "The Neighbourhood Guild," and well expresses the principle on which it is founded. This object, if attained, fills up, or at least bridges over, the gulf between the classes which modern civilization has created, and restores the solidarity of the race.

This uniform principle, worked in different places amidst different circumstances, produces its effects in each case along the lines of least resistance. In most places the neighbours who offer least resistance to the advances of well-meaning friends are children, and the relation which more easily establishes itself between those who have knowledge and those who want it is that of teacher and pupil. This is the reason why the young form so large a proportion of the frequenters of settlements, and why so much of the practical work carried on is educational. As education is the easiest and earliest development of the settlement principle, some people have supposed that the settlements were mere agencies of the University Extension movement; but although those who are active in extending education amongst the people by University teaching find a congenial home and an excellent basis of operation in the settlement, it is a mistake to suppose that education is the main purpose for which settlements are founded, or the object chiefly pursued by the majority of their residents. The friendship first formed with the children goes on naturally to the mothers. It extends from them to the fathers and older members of the family, until the whole circle is drawn into the bond. The friendship begun in the class-room extends itself to the amusements, to the family life, to means for improving the material prosperity of the neighbours, to sociability and friendly discussion, and to the duties and obligations of civic life, until sympathy and brotherly kindness have invaded and conquered the entire life.

In carrying out the uniform principle of beginning by the promotion of neighbourly kindness special difficulties in each place may be encountered. In the American cities, for example, the moment you get beyond the children progress is impeded by the same obstacle as that which stopped the building of the Tower of Babel. There is a confusion of tongues. The proportion of English-speaking poor is small, and the languages spoken by the majority include nearly every one spoken in Europe, as well as Chinese. This not only makes it difficult for residents in the settlements to communicate freely with the people— that might be overcome with comparative ease—but it makes it impossible for the people to communicate with each other. If you call a meeting of the general body of citizens, there is no common language in which it can be addressed. There is a similar difficulty on a much smaller scale from the foreign Jews in Whitechapel, but the insignificant ratio they bear to the rest of the population, and the comparatively small area within which they are to be found, renders the obstacle of no practical importance in British settlements.

So far as the experiment of University Settlement has as yet proceeded, there have been two remarkable and to some extent unexpected results produced upon the residents themselves. In the first place, it is the universal testimony of all settlements in Great Britain and America, that, so far from the case being one in which the wise bestow knowledge upon the simple without return, the teachers themselves have in all cases learnt more than they have taught. Their own views of life have been enlarged, their own errors and prejudices have been corrected, and fresh qualities of the human character for love and admiration have been revealed to them. The class heresies, which the separation of the rich from the neighbourhood of the poor has engendered, have been to some extent removed. They are conscious that their own spiritual and intellectual faculties have been strengthened and their own lives enriched by the broadening of their social sympathies.

The second result is the discovery that the time spent in settlement work, so far from being dull or irksome, is the happiest period of their lives. The interest is unflagging, the torment of *ennui* is unknown, and although sad sights are seen and sad stories heard, there are examples in the lives of the poor of generosity, of kindness, of self-sacrifice, and of devotion to duty which might even reconcile a cynic to the continued existence of the human race.

But the importance of University men and women making friends of the poor has an objective as well as a subjective side ; and I must pass from a consideration of the subjective motives for, and the subjective results of, settlement amongst the poor, to the purposes which such proceedings serve, both as regards the poor themselves and the nation at large.

The social problems of the day are many of them of extreme difficulty and urgency, and cannot be solved by the shouting of demagogues, nor put aside to suit the convenience of partisans. The people who are more directly interested in their speedy and correct solution are the wage-earners themselves, especially that large body of wage-earners whose receipts are below or but little above the starvation point. These are the unskilled, unorganized labourers, who form about five-sixths of the whole body of workers of the United Kingdom. The prevalent political sentiment of such people is apathy. They live from hand to mouth; they have no hope of bettering their condition; they accept such pleasures, sometimes of a very degrading sort, as their present state supplies; and they receive promises of amelioration, which philanthropists or politicians make them, often from interested motives, with scornful incredulity. They have a dull sense of being treated by society with injustice, and a dull rancour against the rich and leisured classes for not inventing some plan by which their condition might be improved. But they have no plan themselves; they have no leaders whom they trust; they have no revolutionary projects to carry out, either by violence or by the legitimate use of their votes. It is a mistake to regard Whitechapel, or the 19th Ward of Chicago, as seething with discontent, and ripe for insurrection and anarchy. The people are capable, as all miserable people are, of being goaded into some sudden and senseless outbreak, but their general state is that of indifference to their economic condition. They will furnish no force for the furtherance of social or political changes unless they are first aroused.

The political philosopher, on the other hand, may attack the social problems of the day in a scientific spirit; he may acquire all the knowledge upon the subject which books, reports, and statistics can impart: but if he remains in his class isolation, if he never comes into personal contact with the people about whom he theorizes, nor estimates by personal experience the forces with which he is dealing, he is no better than a chemist without a laboratory, or an astronomer without a telescope. If, by some lucky accident, he were to hit upon the true solution of some social problem, it would be a barren result, because he would have no force at his disposal to carry the discovery into practical effect.

It is the object of University Settlements to bring together these two impotent factors, and to make out of them an efficient instrument for national progress. There is the latent interest and the latent power in the masses; there is the latent knowledge and the latent ability in the men and women of culture. Make friends and associates of the two parties, and the problems which aré insoluble to each alone become determinable by the two combined. The social questions of the day can be calmly and scientifically examined ; the facts of the case can be accurately ascertained ; the measures to be taken arrived at in accordance with common sense and the general interests of society ; and the keen interest which an instructed and enlightened people would have in their own amelioration would supply the irresistible force necessary to carry such measures into speedy execution.

The objective advantage of University Settlements may be estimated from another point of view. The mass of the workers in the United Kingdom have no organization and no leaders. It is only a small section, not more than one-sixth of the whole, that belongs to trade-unions, and combines more or less perfectly to look after its own interests. The trade-unionists, indeed, as a class, have more sympathy with the unskilled workers than the rich and cultivated sections of society, for the simple reason that they still live nearer to the poor. They have not banished them from their society; there is no great gulf yet fixed between them. But except for their keener sympathy, trade-unionists have no special qualification for deciding on the questions which affect the welfare of the poorer unskilled workers. Even as regards their own trades, the objects they pursue are often economically unsound, and tend to the detriment rather than to the advantage of their members. Good will towards the poor they undoubtedly possess, but knowledge and wisdom are often lacking.

But there are far worse guides than trade-unionists into whose hands the poor may fall. People who are ignorant and wretched are the natural prey of designing persons, who may for their own selfish ends stir them up by promises of social salvation to revolutionary outbreaks. "Superior" people, in discussing labour questions, are never tired of denouncing the perversity of trade-unionists and the wickedness of agitators. But before blaming the poor for following such leaders as they have got, it is surely only reasonable that they should have the opportunity of obtaining sounder advice. If the people had wise counsellors whom they trusted the trade-unionists would gladly accept their co-operation, and take their views into consideration, and the selfish agitators would probably disappear. Such a position University men and women settled amongst the poor have every prospect of attaining. They are not generally wealthy; they do not incur the suspicion of looking upon questions from the capitalist side ; they have no object of their own to serve ; they have better chances than their poorer neighbours of arriving at a right judgment ; and their advice, when the confidence of the people is gained, is likely to be sought and followed.

University Settlements have not been established long enough, and have not yet been widely enough spread, to give any idea of the results which they are capable of producing upon the general condition of modern society. They have scarcely passed beyond the experimental stage. But, so far as results have been obtained, the promoters of the movement have every reason to be satisfied and every encouragement to persevere. A great stimulus to education has been, for the reasons above stated, the earliest and most conspicuous effect of most settlements. It is remarkable that the desire, even of the poorer workers, for knowledge seems to be directed towards abstract science and general culture, rather than towards those studies which could be turned to practical use in manufacturing industry. This is scarcely what would have been expected amongst people who are struggling for their daily bread. The programme of lectures at Toynbee Hall during the present year has embraced history, economics, English, French, German, Italian, Latin and Greek literature, and natural science. Even in Chicago, where the whole city is given to the worship of the dollar, we are told in this year's report that "emphasis is laid upon the humanities, and no attempt is made to supply means for earning a livelihood ; the most popular and continuous courses have

C

been in literature, languages, music, art, history,
mathematics, and drawing." Still more remarkable
is the direction taken by the voluntary clubs and
associations for self-improvement which spring out
of the more formal classes. At Toynbee Hall there
are at the present time antiquarian, economic, Shakespeare, Elizabethan literature, philosophical, natural
history, chemical, and electrical societies. There are
reading associations for studying Cromwell's letters,
Adam Smith, Shakespeare's plays, Browning, and
other English poets. In the yearly prospectus there
is a significant notice that the Greek literature class
is full, and that a supplementary class will have to
be formed. At Hull House, Chicago, the students
have formed an association, divided into the literary,
the dramatic, the musical, and the debating sections.
It meets once a month, and each section in turn is
responsible for an evening's entertainment. The
programme is succeeded by a dance in the gymna-
sium. These facts prove that settlements are not
forcing uncongenial studies upon a reluctant people ;
their difficulty is to keep up with the demand ; and
these so-called " lower classes " show a zeal for self-
improvement, and have acquired an amount of knowledge which might put some of the so-called " higher
classes " to shame.

Next to education, the most conspicuous of the
results attained by settlements is the improvement
and establishment of clubs for men and women, for
boys and girls. Clubs have a beneficent influence
upon the home life of the poor. It is not only that
they take the place of public-houses or saloons as

the place of entertainment of the head of the house-
hold, to the great advantage of the family purse and
of the family tranquillity : that, though an important,
is only a negative advantage. But the club pursuits
of each member of the family—father or son, daughter
or mother—bring new interests into the daily life of
the home. Working-men's clubs are not so exclusive
as those of the West End of London. The families
of their members find ready admission to the entertainments—musical, dramatic, or literary—which the
clubs from time to time provide. The area of friendships is extended by these social gatherings, and the
short period of leisure which the stress of daily toil
allows is pleasantly and usefully employed. It is
declared by those who have watched the effect of
clubs, that the age of marriage in any neighbourhood
is raised by their establishment. If the time has
been too short to test this by statistics, it is easy to
see that there are many influences of club life which
would tend in that direction. For boys' clubs it is
especially claimed that they have a wonderful civilizing effect upon the raw material out of which, if left
to itself, the roughest and most intractable elements
of the future generation would be developed. They
create, it is said, a sort of *esprit de corps*, like that of
the British public schools, under the humanizing
influence of which the most unpromising lad will
acquire self-control, self-respect, and good manners,
and will abstain from unworthy conduct, because he
is afraid of incurring the bad opinion of those whom
he is proud to look upon as his comrades.

The residents in settlements promote good clubs

in two ways—(1) by themselves becoming members of already existing institutions, (2) by founding new ones.

The first method, though more difficult in the commencement, is more effective in the long run. It requires, no doubt, great tact and judgment to leaven the sentiment of a club without the appearance of either presumption or patronage; but every society contains its progressive and improving section, and, if the majority of an independent self-supporting club can be brought to a right way of thinking, the effect is likely to be permanent. The weak point of clubs established by residents themselves is, that they have a tendency always to remain in a state of dependence, and to collapse when the support on which they were built up is withdrawn.

But besides the clubs influenced or established, there are clubs which spring up spontaneously in the settlement neighbourhood. For these the settlement is entitled to take credit, for it is a social and intellectual centre, possessing the character of permanency, about which various enterprises and various organizations for the good of the neighbourhood may group themselves. For example, close by Hull House, Chicago, there has grown up a residential club for young working women, in which fifty girls, earning their living, board and lodge themselves with a comfort and refinement which leaves nothing to be desired. This club gets advice from Hull House, but nothing more. It was originally founded by seven trade-union girls; it has been self-supporting from the first; there is no matron or outside control;

the officers are elected by the members and serve gratuitously ; and the cost to each member is three dollars a week.

The settlements aim at becoming the trusted advisers of the poor ; there is one sort of advice that the poor are most anxious to obtain, and that is legal advice. A poor man who thinks he has a claim, or who conceives himself to have suffered an injustice, is in a condition of perfect helplessness. His comrades are as ignorant of law as himself. He has no hope of obtaining redress, unless he can get some powerful friends to intervene in his behalf. At the University Settlement in Glasgow an effort is made to supply this want. A poor man's lawyer sits there weekly to give advice gratis ; and he has not only given advice, but, when convinced of the justice of the cases, he has either seen his clients through court himself or has handed them over to a poor's agent. At Mansfield House, Poplar, a similar plan is instituted. Two legal members of the settlement sit weekly, to give gratuitous legal advice to all comers. It is said that few cases ever come into court : often the applicant is wholly mistaken, and his grievance exists only in his imagination ; friendly intervention settles many other cases ; and, in the few cases in which legal proceedings should be taken, the name of a good solicitor is given. In American cities the poor, being foreigners, are much more ignorant of their legal · rights and far more helpless in asserting them. The settlements there have thus a peculiarly favourable opportunity of acquiring in this manner the confidence of the poor.

The advice and co-operation of settlements in promoting the organization of labour and directing its objects and methods in accordance with sound economic principles have never been refused. Meetings of trade-unions, both regular and special, have been held in their halls. Workers who were unorganized, and therefore helpless, have been assisted to form unions for their common protection. In America especially, where there are obstacles to joint action, such as diversity of language, many unions owe their existence to the help and advice given at their inception by the residents. Women, who need combination, even more than men, to prevent the reduction of their wages by competition below starvation point, and whose unions have never been accused of intimidation or violence, have found the necessary counsel and assistance in the settlement.

The co-operative movement, full of such immense possibilities in the future to the working classes, is an object in the settlements of careful and anxious study. In Great Britain co-operative distribution is now established. Its operations are already great, its progress is rapid, its ultimate triumph is only a question of time. The problem of the day is how the enormous power of the English and Scottish Co-operative Wholesale Societies, as the greatest purchasers in the United Kingdom, can be best used in promoting the welfare of the producers. Co-operative productive societies have in most cases languished hitherto, partly from inefficient management, but chiefly from the difficulty, amidst the keen commercial competition of the day, of finding a

market for their produce. If the productive societies
worked for orders from the wholesale, the latter
difficulty would be annihilated. Management, when
the workers are by experience made conscious of its
necessity, it is not difficult to provide. Practical
steps in this direction have already been taken by
the settlements, and in most cases with excellent
results, and the further development of co-operation will find admirable helpers amongst them. In
American cities the poor are much less thrifty than
in this country, and even co-operative distribution is
still almost unknown. Both in New York and Chicago
the settlements have formed co-operative societies,
in the former for the distribution of dairy products,
in the latter for the provision of fuel. This is done
for the purpose of teaching the people the advantage of co-operation, and in the expectation that
the principle will be adopted by them and further
developed.

In civic life there is an immense field for instruction, for advice, and for action. In the United
Kingdom the functions of government, both Imperial
and local, are performed by professional officials,
trained to the service, and naturally jealous of having
their operations interfered with in an irregular manner
by outsiders. But the scheme of the British Local
Government requires the co-operation with the permanent officials of a number of elected persons who
represent the wishes and even the prejudices of the
people. The difficulty in a district inhabited almost
exclusively by the poor is to find persons fit to be
elected to perform these duties. The poor themselves

have neither knowledge nor leisure for such service, nor can they meet the expense, small as it may be. Elective offices thus fall in many places into the hands of persons who exploit them for their own pecuniary ends. This gives rise to that jobbery which is not unknown amongst local authorities in the United Kingdom, and to the shameful corruption called "boodling," which is the curse of local self-government in many of the great cities of America. The University Settlements supply the poorer neighbourhoods which cannot find candidates of their own with persons ready to serve on the local boards, who bring to their task scrupulous honesty and a sincere desire to do their duty by those whom they represent. Besides serving as members of the local authority there is a great opening for usefulness in the organization of vigilant committees to see that the laws which already exist for the protection of the poor are carried into actual effect. In all times and in all countries it is much easier to make laws than to enforce them. Many of those now on the statute book of the United Kingdom, which are pointed to with exultation by partisans as proofs of the benevolence of their party, are practically a dead letter. I have heard it stated as an admitted fact, at a meeting of all the University Settlements in East London, that if a weekly tenant complains of the insanitary condition of his house he receives immediate notice to quit, and if he owes any rent the brokers are at once put in. Under such circumstances some of the settlements have established vigilance committees, composed chiefly of the workers themselves, who stir up the authorities in cases of bad drains, neglected cesspools, damp floors and walls, leaky roofs, and fever dens.

In America, where the public service is not professional, there is much less jealousy of outside interference, and much more readiness on the part of local authorities to accept the assistance of volunteers. It is on this account that, though the duration of settlements has been shorter than in Great Britain, their effects in public life have been more conspicuous. Hull House, Chicago, managed by women under the leadership of Miss Jane Addams, and carried on on the same principles as the British settlements, has operated for five years only. At an early stage the residents began an investigation into the condition of child labour, and their revelation of the extent to which children were sacrificed to the exigencies of cheap manufacture, backed up by their friends amongst the trade-unionists, compelled the State Government to intervene. At the instance of Miss Kelly, a resident of Hull House, a bill was introduced into the Illinois Legislature regulating the hours and conditions of labour of women and children. A committee of investigation, sent down by the State Government to inspect sweetshops and decide on the necessity for legislation, was piloted by her on its tour, and when the law was passed she was appointed Inspector of Factories in the State of Illinois. The same lady has been also appointed by the Department of Labour at Washington to conduct in Chicago a so-called "slum investigation." A club of young factory women has been formed, which meets at Hull House, to propagate information respecting the new law, and to form vigilance committees for the purpose of securing that the eight-hours day, to which the labour of women in the State of Illinois is now restricted, shall be observed. The settlement has also formed a 19th Ward Improvement Club, which meets monthly at Hull House. The president is the district representative in the Illinois State Legislature, and one of the ward aldermen is an active member. The club is pledged to the improvement of the ward in all directions. It has standing committees in street-cleaning, etc., and has been largely instrumental in inducing the city council to erect for the inhabitants of the ward a free public bath-house, which is now in daily use.

In the City of New York, where settlements are still more recent, the same kind of work is being pushed on. A "Clean City League" has been formed, which has published handbills in many languages, urging upon the people the civic duty of taking proper means for disposal of refuse, the mischief of casting papers and banana-peels about, the necessity of teaching habits of cleanliness in the streets to their children. There is a "Tenth Ward Social Reform Club," with an "anti-sweating section." This section has been addressing itself to the enforcement of that part of the law of New York State which prohibits the employment of garment-workers in any part of a dwelling-house. The members of the section obtained the co-operation of the officials of the Jewish Tailors' Union and of the Knee Pants Makers' Union, and they carried on the work in concert with the factory inspectors. The process adopted was a visit, a warning, and a report to the inspector. Beyond this it has never been found necessary to proceed ; the law has been complied with. Conferences are also held of the public school teachers in the Tenth Ward, under the auspices of this Reform Club, in which such subjects as the home, school, and street life of children are discussed, and the best methods of inculcating good behaviour and civic duty. The residents also took an active part in the recent successful movement for delivering the city of New York from the Tammany ring, and the corruption, inefficiency, and extravagance by which its adminis· tration was marked, and they have impressed upon the citizens "that municipal government shall be entirely divorced from party politics and from selfish personal ambition and gain, and that the economical, honest, and business-like management of public affairs has nothing to do with questions of National or State policy."

I have given at some length, but I hope without too great a tax on the patience of my readers, some details of what has already been effected here and in America by the principle of social intercourse between the Universities and the poor. I have done so because the propensity of British people is always to distrust theories, and to look—sometimes prematurely, some-times, perhaps, too exclusively — at results. The examples which I have given are only specimens of the good deeds of University Settlements ; some of the best have, I dare say, been omitted. But even judged by results, after so short a trial, and upon so imperfect a catalogue of their achievements, I think it will be admitted that University Settlements have been a great success in the past, and are full of hope for the future.

In conclusion, I will state summarily the propositions which I regard as established :—

1. That great city areas inhabited nearly exclusively by wage-earners, from which those who possess wealth, leisure, or culture are withdrawn, are a new phenomenon produced by modern civilization.

2. That in these cities of the poor a large and probably increasing proportion of the population, neither criminals nor loafers, is unable with the utmost industry to earn a living wage.

3. That this state of things is discreditable to our Christianity and civilization, and is dangerous to the stability of our present social system.

4. That public subscriptions of money to relieve the periodic aggravations of a state of poverty and misery which is chronic, so far from mitigating, only aggravate the evil.

5. That the Universities, as representing the highest wisdom and knowledge of the nation, are under a moral obligation to attempt the difficult task of discovering a cure for this social disease.

6. That the method adopted by the University Settlements, of basing the investigation of the evils and their remedies upon the cultivation of friendly social relations with the various classes of workers, is the true method by which the solution of the problem should be approached.

7. That the results of University Settlement, so far as they have gone, both here and in America, are in themselves good, and give every encouragement for the further development of the system upon the lines upon which these results have been obtained.

WORKING MEN'S CLUBS

BY

THE REV. A. F. WINNINGTON INGRAM

HEAD OF THE OXFORD HOUSE, BETHNAL GREEN

WORKING MEN'S CLUBS.

LET us be quite clear at starting. This paper is on working-men's clubs of a certain sort. There have been working men's clubs existing in East London for many years ; most of them are formed for political objects on the one side or the other, and in all of them, so far as I know, drink is sold. I have nothing special to say of these in the present paper ; let those who know more of them attack them, if they wish to do so, and let those who manage them defend them.

What I am about to describe is an effort to promote the foundation of other clubs in the district which shall be equally democratic and, if possible, equally self-supporting, but which shall aim at an altogether higher ideal of club life. There are some who think that the best way to raise the club life of the district is for right-minded men to join as individuals existing clubs, and all honour to the men who have the patience for such work ; but their work, so far from being hindered, will be materially helped by an object-lesson near at hand of what club life may be ; and such an object-lesson, if it can be effectively given, is a quicker agent in accomplishing what all have at heart, than the other slower method by itself.

D

What, then, are the special characteristics of the
new sort of working men's clubs, which have "caught
on" so much in East London and elsewhere during
the past ten years?

I. In the first place they have no intoxicants
sold in them at all. We admit, that at first, this
sounds narrow-minded, and likely to defeat the very
object of a working men's club by keeping out the
working men; but experience often reverses the most
plausible *a priori* theories, and undoubtedly the popularity of the clubs which have this rule, always
supposing the club life in them is bright and attractive, shows that large numbers of working men in
a place like East London are only too thankful to
be "out of the drink" altogether; while from a club
point of view, the comparative absence of quarrelling,
the indefinable difference of tone, and the popularity
of the club with the "missus" are gains only to be
seen to be realized. "Do you mind John giving us
so much of his company at the Club?" I ask my
lady friends in Bethnal Green. "No, sir, *I knows
where he is*"—an answer the significance of which is
the greater the longer one has lived in the district.

II. Then the second characteristic is the stern
refusal of any political test. Politics and political
clubs are all very well in their way, but the political
test gives an essentially narrow basis for club life.
If you want to have a good club, you must have
plenty of life, and the more variegated the opinions
and the freer the intermingling of men of all kinds,
the fuller the life of the club. Take the debates
alone; how much more lively it is for the members

to have both sides represented, and to rub shoulders
in a keen and friendly way with men who differ
from one another in opinion as widely as the poles.
Naturally in a district where the population is largely
of one political colour, the debates will be one-sided
in any clubs, and I have seen the House of Lords
swept away nightly like driftwood on the waves, and
the Church disestablished once a week; but I have
also seen in the same clubs, on some occasions, "con-
tracting out" left by a majority in the Employers'
Liability Bill, and the Church saved by the skin of
its teeth.

It is not merely, however, the debates which the
abolition of political tests improves, it enlarges the
whole scope of the club, which then becomes a combination of men as men to live a truer man's life.
Freed from the incubus of running a political programme, it can turn its attention to the social and
physical condition of the district in which it is
situated; it can have its sanitary committee in connection with the Mansion House Council; it can run
its co-operative stores; it can try the experiment of
a bookshop; get together a good library; organize
sub-societies for every sort of sport and recreation—
football, cricket, cycling, rowing, running, chess, gymnastics, whist; and, last but not least, can develop a
clay-pipe club, to settle, amid the fumes of tobacco,
the deepest problems which beset the social reformer.

In connection with the University Club, which is
in my mind as I write, with its membership of eight
hundred working men, there is also a sick fund, a loan
society, a penny bank, a choral society, two bands

(string and brass), a Shakespeare club, and a flourishing dramatic society and, in connection with it, an institute for young men who will eventually join it at the age of twenty-one; there is also a children's club, consisting entirely of the children of its members.

There is, indeed, no reason why a club of this description should not be a "University" in something more than name. As the intellectual interest is gradually fostered under the influence of lectures, debates, a good reading-room, and branches of the Home Reading Union, there is a possibility for intellectual teaching to be given in the future by the University Extension Society or other bodies, to an extent only limited by the intellectual interest of its members, while the physical life, which receives at the Universities so full a recognition and development, is being already developed in a way that bids fair to rival the energy of Oxford herself. Last year was not the first time that a Bethnal Green club four has defeated a four from Oxford, nor do the West by any means always come off victorious in "five hundred up" at billiards.

III. But, after all, a university aims at more than intellectual education and physical recreation, and I, for one, should always hold that a club fell far short of its possible ideal if it made no provision for the religious life; and no one, therefore, with any experience will wonder that a first essential is the abolition of any religious test. I am not denying for a moment that many clergy are perfectly justified in having clubs with religious tests. Why should they not? A clergyman has, perhaps, limited accommodation;

he has room, we will say, for one hundred men and
no more : he has one hundred men communicants
or one hundred in a Bible-class ; why should not
they have some amusement, because they happen to
be religious ?   He is perfectly justified, if he thinks
it best for his parish, in handing over his club-rooms
to be the play-rooms for his guild or Bible-class. My
only point is, that the club ceases to be a missionary
agency in the cause of light and truth in its action
on its own members ; it is a tent for the peaceful
Jacob, not a shaft let down into the manhood of the
jolly but non-religious Esau. They are two distinct
methods of working : in the one case, you carefully
tame your human animal, and then turn him into
green pastures ; in the other case, "you take the
human animal as you find him, and touch him at
any point he can be touched."   And therefore it
stands to reason that "no religious test" is as
essential to such a club as I am attempting to
describe, as "no political test," or a "no drink."   To
have a club looked on as "a parson's trap," to button-
hole for Bible-classes as you go round the billiard-
rooms, to be thought "to have a card up your sleeve"
in any dealings with the members, is to court failure.
A man, when he has paid his entrance fee, and been
duly elected, must be as free to come and go, and
do what he likes in the club, so long as he conforms
to the rules, as a bishop is free to come and go and
do what he likes at the Athenæum : no one thinks of
button-holing a bishop in the Athenæum to become
a member of the Land League as a condition of
membership, and a working man is rightly insulted

if he finds that there are conditions of his club other than are " in the bond."

But all this is merely clearing the ground for the true influence, which is the perfectly natural and legitimate influence of man on man. It is an impossible thing that any one with strong Christian faith can be knit up with a body of men year in and year out, through happiness, through trouble, in the midst of all the ups and downs of life, without imparting in some measure his faith. Surface prejudice and surface shyness go down before the stress and trouble of life, but they also go down before the daily and hourly intercourse of men with one another in all the common work and common interest of club life; club Bible-classes may be formed, a Sunday service may be held in the club hall, and club services may be held quarterly, in one of the churches of the district, such as the gathering of the clans which meets, under a banner with Oxford on one side of it and Bethnal Green on the other, every quarter, in one of the churches of the district.

But it is time now to descend more completely from the abstract to the concrete; this ideal is all very well, it may be said, but is it anywhere else but "laid up in heaven," like Plato's ideal republic? if in working order, how does it pay its way? what is the actual method of management? and is it possible to point to any results of the experiment?

Let us take these questions in order. Every one knows how long an experiment has to be tested in a place like East London before it can be definitely said to have answered the expectations formed with regard to it ; but still ten years cannot be considered a mere moment even down here, and it was ten years ago that the Oxford House Club was founded. It began in a very small way, and it is still one of the jokes of the club, among the older members, to recall the mingled curiosity and apprehension with which they crept round the corner in which the disused schoolroom was situated, which was to be their first club premises, and came to see what the " Oxford gents" were up to by their invitation. That club was founded on precisely the lines indicated above ; it has held together in spite of seeing younger clubs spring up round it with far grander premises ; it has kept its central core of old members who have been devoted to it from the start ; and it has never been more flourishing than at the present time, when, 250 strong, it is entering the new club buildings this winter for which it has waited for ten long years, and which will enable it to expand its membership to 500.

A few years later was founded the University Club, of which mention has been already made. It was started first in a little back street, with a membership of sixteen ; then, under the fostering care of Mr. P. R. Buchanan, who at that time joined the Oxford House Settlement, it made two more successive jumps, and in a few years found itself in spacious buildings in Victoria Park Square, with a membership of over a thousand. The establishment of the teetotum clubs in Ratcliffe, Whitechapel, Shoreditch, Hackney, Stamford Hill, and elsewhere, with memberships varying from a hundred to five hundred members, by a perfectly natural process reduced the membership to eight hundred, as men who had come for miles to the University at first, naturally did not continue to do so when they found a somewhat similar club by their own door. We may presume, then, that the membership has now found its natural level in eight hundred ; and, indeed, except from a financial point of view, a club of eight hundred men members, with all the institutions in connection with their wives and children which centre round it, is quite as large as you want, if you are to keep up a spirit of mutual friendship and a real *esprit de corps.*

And here, without trenching upon the ground of my two colleagues, Mr. Legge and Mr. Fiennes, I must say a word on the importance of having men's clubs "fed from below." It is a great help to any men's club, to have a constant succession every year of some fifty or sixty young members, already trained in a boys' club or young men's institute to understand club life, already accustomed to serve on committees, to suppress themselves for the good of the community, and yet giving that constant supply of young life which helps to keep a club from going to sleep. Such feeders we have in the "University Institute," which feeds the University Club ; and the Webbe Institute, of nearly four hundred boys, which feeds the Oxford House Club : and such an additional feeder we hope to have in the future in the club which Mr. Legge himself has managed so admirably, and which is now launched on its career, in the name of Repton School, as the "Repton Club."

So, again, with regard to the federation of which Mr. Fiennes will speak. I must not be understood to write as if Oxford House was the only agency throughout London in starting such clubs as I have described : many of the sixty clubs now federated to the House have been avowedly started in direct imitation of our clubs, as was stated in very generous terms at the conference to which this book owes its start; but many clergy, most college and school missions, and some independent workers were all making experiments in the same direction, and "the Federation" is an attempt to give the strength of combination to the whole effort throughout London.

But, secondly, granted that it is a real working experiment, how does a club like this pay its way? And we must admit at once that, up to now, such clubs have always required an initial outlay of capital in the buildings and in the plant. There is, however, no inherent reason why this should always be the capital of a philanthropic outsider. Once let the working men of London realize that these clubs are the things to "go for" from the point of view of their own enjoyment,—once let them realize, as they are beginning to do, that you get more for your money in every way than you get in a public-house, and that what is good for them is also good for others, and we shall have these clubs started by the workers themselves with co-operative capital; and it is possible that, if we fail to do it in London, the Northerners themselves will step in and show us the way, as they have done with the whole co-operative movement. At first, however, there is little matter of surprise that a new thing has needed at the start backing from the outside.

Nor need we feel disheartened that the working expenses are not yet wholly satisfactory. I have before me the balance sheets for 1893, both for the Oxford House Club and for the University Club. I find that the former, paying a weekly subscription of 1½d., an entrance fee on new members of 6d., and with an average paying membership of 230, has paid its way completely with a balance of £10 to spare, but up to now it has had the use of its premises rent free. Similarly, the University Club, with a membership of 800, and subscriptions 1d. a week, and entrance fee 1s., gives an account of the £851 which they have received and expended. Subscriptions and nominations amount to £173, receipts from billiards and bagatelle £326, receipts from entertainments £242 ; while the principal expenses are wages £288, rates and taxes £118, gas and water £262. There is a balance of 18s. 6½d., but here, again, the £150 allowed for rent has not been paid.

It is only fair, however, to say that for three years, when the membership was over a thousand, before the competition of the clubs started as copies of it began, the club paid its rent as well as its other expenses ; and during that time was in the proud position of the only large working men's club in London which paid its way without the sale of intoxicating drink. One of two things would make it pay its way again : if the membership were to rise, matters would right themselves ; but if it does not, the course is always open to raise the subscription from 1d. to 1½d. or 2d. a week. Whether this would affect the membership is an interesting question.

3. Thirdly, let us tackle the question of management, on which so much depends. And here it is not altogether easy to steer between the Scylla of despotism and the Charybdis of anarchy. Many clubs split upon the rock of despotism : the members find that they have no free voice in their own affairs ; it is not *their* club ; it is somebody's else club run for them ; they cease to take any interest in it, and often leave it altogether. On the other hand, there have been not a few instances of gallant ships, left to steer themselves too soon, which have been swept into the whirlpool of anarchy, and have never been seen again.

The first essential for a good club, is a nucleus of enlightened working men, who are keen to raise, if only a little, the standard of life in their district. It is by getting a few of these together, and, if necessary, impregnating them with something of this spirit, that an outsider of rather better education than themselves may be of great assistance. It may either be a layman who will come to reside in the working-class quarter, or, failing a good layman, the clergyman of the parish. After a few good men have been got together, and some sort of premises secured in which to make a start, it may be necessary, for the first year, that these few should be a kind of preliminary and tentative committee ; but as soon as the members once enter into the spirit of the thing, then the club must become frankly democratic. The principles of the club, such as were described at the beginning of this paper, can be safeguarded by being vested, as at the University

Club, in a council with the power of veto ; this council should hold also all the property in its name, except what may be hereafter bought with the money of the members, and this can be entered on a separate inventory. Short of the violation of these principles, of (a) no intoxicating drink, (b) no political test, (c) no religious test, and, in the case of our own clubs, (d) that they are branches of the Oxford House, the members must be left entirely free to manage their own affairs. At a general meeting, held quarterly or half-yearly, the club will choose its committee of twelve or eighteen, according to its size, for the year, changing sometimes half the members of it every half-year, the old members being always eligible for re-election.

This committee, once elected, will have absolute power to enforce the rules and regulations of the club which will have been passed in full general meeting, to keep order, admit members, and generally manage the club. One of its members will be "chairman for the week," and, though there is always an appeal from the committee to a special general meeting on the requisition of a certain specified number of members, it is a sign of a good club to respect the decisions of its committee, which it has itself elected, at any rate until the end of its term of office, when it can be—and often is—"hauled over the coals" to any extent by discontented members.

I have been present at some very stormy general meetings, but, so far from regarding them with any apprehension, I look on them as a sign of life.

Anything is better than stagnation in a club, and a little fire in a general meeting is a sign that members care for what is going on, and a keen competition for places on the committee is another sure sign of life.

Knotty points arise from time to time. I remember that, some five years ago, when I was in the chair, at a large committee meeting of the University Club, some eight members, during the dock strike, appeared, hot and angry, demanding that eight others should be turned out of the club because they had "gone in as blacklegs" that morning. The rule cited, under which the demand was made, stated that members who "injured fellow-members of the club" were subject to expulsion. The difficulty of the question consisted in this—that the rule contemplated personal injury in the club itself. The club was distinctly formed on a purely social basis, apart from politics and from labour disputes, and yet it was hard to say that the eight members had not, in a certain sense "injured" the interests of the others. The difficulty, however, was solved by the members of the committee, nearly all of whom were keen trade-unionists, deciding, by a large majority, that it was not a matter of which they could take notice consistently with maintaining the special character of the club—a decision which will be regarded by most men, whatever their views on the subject of "blacklegs," as showing a considerable amount of self-restraint and cool-headedness at a time of great excitement.

And, indeed, as I turn to face the last question —What results can you definitely name as a result of this ten years' experiment ?—I should feel inclined to put first and foremost (*a*) the astonishing education in self-government which a club, worked in such a way as I have described, gives to its members, and especially to its committee. The unselfish and unpaid work demanded of them, the grip of a new ideal to work for beyond the immediate necessities of daily life, the development of powers of organization and management which long have been dormant for want of use, end by turning out, after some years, men whom you would readily trust with your life or your honour, and who would be well fitted, if opportunity offered, for posts of high responsibility in municipal and civil life.

(*b*) Then, secondly, we may note, as an undoubted effect of club life of this satisfying sort, the raising of the ordinary age of marriage among the younger members of the clubs. As the "club parson," who is generally invited by the bride and bridegroom— and allowed by the unfailing courtesy of the surrounding clergy—to bring to a happy termination an engagement of which he has long been in the secret, I have special opportunities for testing this, and I am never now asked to tie the irrevocable knot until the bridegroom is at least twenty-five ; whereas, if I come across a boy who has "dropped out" between the boys' club and the men's club, or for some other reason has "turned up the club," I almost invariably find that he has married at nineteen or twenty.

It is not difficult to see how this result would come about. The young man who stays in the club is thoroughly comfortable of an evening, and does not feel the want of a "home of his own," like the other; and, more than this, his standard of comfort and his idea of what a man's life ought to be rise every year; his growth of self-respect increases also his respect for his young woman, and he does not care to marry till he can bring her to where things are a bit tidy, and that means waiting till he (and she, too, if possible) has saved money.

(c) And this brings me to a third undoubted result of such clubs, and that is their civilizing and refining influence. In the boys' club, we always regard as the first proof that the club has begun its work when we hear one boy say to another, "Go and wash your face, you dirty little brute!" for it shows that both the members have come under the power of a public opinion which makes for cleanliness, and which becomes as strong as the public opinion of a good school. Similarly, there soon grows up in a men's club a public opinion in the matter of dress and manners. It is not rude to mention this, for members will mention it themselves. "Rather a difference in the club to seven or eight years ago, sir," said a young club member, as I sat on his bed in the London Hospital, as he was recovering from a terrible illness.

"What do you specially mean?" I asked.

"Well, I, for one, never used to wear a collar, nor did lots of the others; but now *we're quite a decent lot of chaps!*"

"I should think you were," I replied; "any one would take you for regular mashers. How do you manage to look so smart, when I know what your wages are?"

"It is simply this. When a chap has been in a club like ours for a year or two, he has got some money to buy a coat with."

Nor is this an isolated instance of the way in which a bright, attractive club diverts the silver stream from places into which it might otherwise flow. "How is Mr. —— and Mr. ——?" asked a publican whom I was visiting one day, also in a hospital, when he had broken his leg.

"Pretty well," I said; "but how do you know them?"

"Oh, they were regular customers of mine before they joined your club. I kept a house close down your way."

"Are you there now?" I asked.

"No, sir, I've moved *a little further off.*"

After all, it is fair competition. Instead of wasting breath in abusing publicans, many of whom are decent, well-behaved citizens, it is far better, openly and fairly to cut them out, if you can. If the devil is not to have all the best tunes, why should he have all the best games and the brightest rooms in the district?

(*d*) But what, it may be asked, are the results on the home life of the members? Much of it goes without saying. If a man becomes more unselfish, more self-controlled, more thrifty, and an habitually sober man, it goes without saying that he is a better father, brother, or son at home; but, in addition to that, the manifold activities of a good club are perpetually reflecting brightness in the home life. As

I visit round of an afternoon, and perhaps take a dish of tea with the missus, I find the girls, as they work, practising snatches of a chorus for the choral society; I find the boy as keen as mustard, as he puts the stitches into the boots his father is making, about the cricket match on Saturday; and the man himself is either hurrying up to play the trombone in the club band, or is getting ready his speech as he finishes his chair (for boots and cabinets are our staple trade), to astonish the natives in the debating society that evening.

(e) And if, as a last question, it may be asked, What are the results from the point of view of a Christian missionary? I can only reply that, to any one who realizes what is the real nature of the problem we have in hand, the extreme slowness with which any one reverses the habits of a lifetime, the complete misapprehension and suspicion with which the Church and even Christianity itself has been regarded, the active propaganda of secularist ideas in workshops, the identification in the minds of many of Christianity with Calvinism, the extremely shady doings of some professed representatives of religion in the district, the results of so short an experiment have been results for which we can thank God.

Much prejudice and suspicion is broken down; lectures in the halls and in the open air, followed by questions and discussions, have done their work, chiefly because the confidence of the listeners has been first gained in the clubs; secularism is largely discredited; Bible smashing is becoming bad form; ordinary Church may be at present too long, but at

E

club service a shortened form of morning prayer becomes a form of service, printed in a little paper book, at once intelligent and popular. A mission service of an hour in the club hall every Sunday sees club members, with their wives and the children, whom the walls of no church or chapel have seen yet ; and a little, steadfast guild of those who, after much thought and some self-sacrifice, wish to be communicant members of the Church, all of whom have found in the club their first step into a Christian atmosphere : these things may be reckoned at once as results of the past, and foretastes of what yet may be in store in the future for working men's clubs.

HOSPITALITIES

BY

THE REV. CANON BARNETT

WARDEN OF TOYNBEE HALL, WHITECHAPEL

HOSPITALITIES.

HOSPITALITY is a duty enforced by experience as well as by command. It is the best expression of good will, the outward and manifest sign of the inward feeling of respect and sympathy. It is the gift which most nearly rises to the level of sharing, the giver making himself one with the receiver, whom he takes into his own home. It is the means by which West End society holds itself together, and every season the army of the classes in possession is welded by dinners and parties.

Host and guest have a peculiar relation. They have eaten salt together, and, if nothing higher is developed, the savage instinct remains to keep them from lifting up hostile hands.

Hospitality was, in old days, if not the secret, then, to a large extent, the source of the power of the chief. The feudal lord entertained his followers and welcomed strangers. The master was the host of his apprentices, and national events were marked by feasts in which all shared. They thus met, as it were, off their guard. They learnt to know one another's thoughts and manners, they discovered points of likeness, and came into quiet possession of a common inheritance.

Modern developments have changed all this. The cash nexus has taken the place of the personal nexus, and leaders hold their followers through their interests. The rich have tastes and habits which are shocked by contact with those of the poor. They live secluded, and every year build up new barriers of luxury. They have probably as much good will to the poor as their fathers had, they are willing to show that good will in gifts as generous, but they cannot endure rough manners and coarse language. They give, but they will not share; they send their money, but keep themselves and their homes behind servants, conventionalities, and high walls.

The two nations of which Disraeli wrote become more and more evident in the nation. The cleavage in the world tends to become horizontal and not vertical. On one side are the classes in possession, who rejoice in their refinements and restraints, in the cleanliness of their persons and the order of their meals, in their knowledge and culture. On the other side are the working classes, who rejoice in their strength, make merry over the mincing ways of their neighbours, and grow angry over what seems to be their hypocrisy and selfishness. Each side is strengthened by hospitality within its own limits. The city of London is an instance how a class in possession may make itself strong. The city abounds in what may be called abuses, but largely by means of its hospitalities it has protected these abuses from reform. The rich are wise in their generation when they spend much time in parties—they make their side strong thereby; the poor do not neglect the same means, as any one may understand who watches the tramcars and railways on Sundays, and marks how great is the interchange of hospitality.

The two nations, that of the rich and that of the poor, are very evident. Each grows strong, and the danger of collision is the great danger of our time. The question of questions is how to make peace and good will, and the question set me to answer in this paper is, How may hospitality serve this end ?

At no time have efforts to do good been more common. It seems to need only a suggestion to create a society, and it is not, therefore, surprising to find that much is being done by the rich to entertain and amuse the poor. Entertainment and amusement were characteristic of old hospitality—the good food and the hearty laugh were measurable gains of the guest. When, therefore, it occurred to the rich of modern time that the poor missed the hospitality of old time, the obvious remedy seemed a supply of entertainment and amusement. What was done feebly by the effort of an individual should now be done with the appliances at the command of an age used to work on a grander scale.

Entertainment societies have been started. Men and women able to sing, to recite, or act, associate themselves together, hire a hall, and give a performance to which the poor are invited or admitted at only a small fee. When they happen to be engaged or to feel tired, their place is supplied by professionals, and the secretary of the society finds that such occasions increase.

Employers — even limited companies — have

adopted the custom of a yearly feast. The works are stopped, a train is hired, and the whole establishment is borne to some hotel at some well-known place. A good dinner is spread, and drink is abundant. At the head of the table sits one of the partners or directors. He has travelled down comfortably, but he appears at the dinner and makes a speech, modelled on what might have been said by a merchant or landlord of old days. He appeals to the sentiment of old ties and common employment. He calls the unskilled labourers friends, and deprecates the breaking of such family relations by a strike. One of the guests replies in the same strain, all cheer and separate for a year.

Every church and chapel has become a centre of treats and teas. The clergy and the staff are busy during the winter organizing tea-parties or entertainments for mother's meetings, clubs, classes, and schools, and during the summer they are as busy organizing excursions for the same people. They by such means get into closer contact with those who attend their ministry, and they do give much pleasure. The clergy have undoubtedly risen in popular estimation by such acts ; they are recognized as being at any rate useful in the things of this world. Some of the winter's parties where the hosts are many and the guests few and well known,—some of the summer excursions where the destination is the house or garden of a friend, who treats the poor as he treats the rich, and where the guests are closely bound by ties of knowledge and respect, have made happy memories in the minds of many.

The same, however, cannot be said of those parties where the contractor's meanness has struggled against the guests' greed, and where the chief duty of the host has been to prevent pocketing ; or of those excursions when the only triumph has been the successful transport of one of " the biggest parties " ever carried from London to the country. The very advertisement of those parties is a reproach. The name of hospitality is taken in vain when a clergyman or missionary appeals for money to take out five hundred or a thousand "slum children," and then gathers the children at the street corners, giving most to those who scramble most, setting a premium on rags and truancy. The account of such a treat in the *Daily News* made painful reading. The children commenced by fighting in the railway carriages ; they rushed wildly about the fields, seeking what to injure and what to devour ; they were fed as beasts are fed ; and they returned shouting and shrieking, intoxicated with excitement, prepared in after life to enjoy the intoxication of a more dangerous stimulant.

Entertainment societies, employers' feasts, the parsons' parties are the appliances by which our generation has tried to supply the place of the hospitality of old days. They seem to do all which our fathers attempted, and to do it more effectively. If the pleasure of hospitality was food, then better food is now more abundantly given ; if the pleasure was in the entertainment, then better entertainment is now provided. A machine is stronger than a man ; it does what he cannot do : and machine hospitality has surpassed any efforts in his power.

This is true, and the movement in favour of amusing the people is to be welcomed. Great good has come of the provision of fine music; and many men and women in an excursion have learnt to value the country sufficiently to seek it again by their own efforts. Great good, too, follows the common meal and the expression of good fellowship. The present age has appliances greater than those possessed by any former age, and it is more disposed to use them for the public good. There is much more wanting to be done in the same direction, and the hope may be encouraged that such places as the Crystal Palace may be carried on at the public expense for the entertainment of Londoners.

But, and this "but" is a very big one, it must be remembered that entertainment is not hospitality, even when it includes feeding and amusement. There are things—perhaps the best things—which a machine cannot do, and no machine—no organization of forces —can exercise hospitably.

The members of an entertainment society may give the best music, they may raise much laughter, they may receive a hearty vote of thanks, but they have not given the hearers the pleasure they give the guests whom they receive in their own rooms and whose visits they return.

The merchant or landlord may provide the most sumptuous repast in a grander room than his own house contains; he may express words of welcome: but somehow his guests will not feel as they feel when, on Sunday, they sit round a neighbour's tea-table; they will not, in the breaking of bread, get the revelation of another being which makes life seem larger.

And the parson's parties—generously provided —do not provoke that generosity of feeling which follows hospitality ; the guests are half conscious that he is only doing his duty, and rewarding them for their attendance at classes or meetings.

Modern efforts at entertainments have their uses and their abuses, but they do not reach the ends of hospitality. They are gifts which do not rise to the level of sharing ; they do not make at one giver and receiver ; they do not reveal the thoughts and manners of his home ; they do not provoke a sense of common possession by interest in one another's possessions : they do little, therefore, to increase peace and good will between the nation of the poor and the nation of the rich.

University Settlements claim to show a way of entertainment which is more nearly hospitality. Settlements, indeed, were, in the first place, started as a protest against the control of philanthropy by machinery. It was never assumed that they would take the place of churches, of organizations, and of societies. It was only claimed that they would provide the hand work—the personal touch—which no machine can supply. They were, therefore, started without the equipment of an endowment, and without any sectarian or political object. They were to be simply club-houses, in which men and women of the university status would live their own lives in the midst of industrial districts. The residents would, it was expected, take their part as citizens and neighbours in the local government and social life of the district. They would be representatives of the various views which hold in religion and politics, and they would be beholden to no body of subscribers or patrons for their support. They, as members of local boards, or in connection with Churches, societies, or clubs, would take their part in fitting institutions to needs, and they would form friendships by the accidents of frequent contact.

The first intention has been modified by circumstances. Some settlements have now been attached to missions, and some have become identified with sectarian objects. The residents have tended to look upon themselves as missionaries, sent to do good works, and not merely as neighbours, living to know and to be known, with shoulders to bear other burdens, and with burdens for other shoulders to bear. Whatever may be the advantage of this development, for other ends, it is well to remember that the first object of a settlement is to bring people together, to promote the contact by which virtue passes from human being to human being, to allow of the personal touch which breaks down the barriers made strong by fear or suspicion.

A settlement, as originally designed, is thus well fitted to be a centre of hospitality. It is perhaps the one large house of the neighbourhood—the one house in which it is possible to enjoy social life. The hired hall—even when it is decorated by the upholsterer—has never the same power over the guests as the home with its marks of daily pleasures and occupations. The residents have, therefore, at

their hands the means of hospitality : they may ask
two or three guests to their own rooms—asking them
to drop in for an hour after work—to eat, drink, and
smoke, as over the fire they chat about the affairs of
the neighbourhood ; and they may invite to the large
common rooms a larger party of their friends, to meet
at dinner, or supper, or for an evening's talk. The
residents of a settlement are thus able to share their
homes and themselves, they are able at once to
make their neighbours feel at one with unaccustomed
surroundings and strange fellow-citizens. They are
able to use their friendship as a means of widening
the sympathies of their friends, and they are able
to use their powers of hospitality to bind their friends
together.

But examples of what has been done may be
more convincing than theories of what is possible.
Obviously very little can be said about the use made
of private rooms. Residents who make friends in
the neighbourhood entertain and are entertained.
The intercourse which they enjoy, and the effect of
that intercourse on character and action, are sacred
from description. It is sufficient to say that those
who live in settlements do ask to their rooms those
whom they learn to know in clubs, in committees,
or at meetings, and are in turn asked again. A very
small effort of imagination is necessary to realize
what follows from such meetings—the mutual respect, the acceptance of other points of view, the
kindling of enthusiasm for reform. Tyrants have
been well advised in preventing by curfew bells the
evening chats, when men of ideas pass on their

thoughts to men of action. The conditions of modern society, which separate thinkers and workers, prevent such chats ; and a settlement which makes them possible is doing something to overthrow a tyranny more powerful than that of Norman conquerors.

Where two or three gather in earnestness and simplicity, there, in a very real sense, is the Christ with His power to convince of righteousness and of sin. And inasmuch as a man's environment is part of himself, no man ever meets another so truly as in the room where he has lived and worked. The resident in a settlement, who has made his room his home, furnished it with his favourite books and pictures, marked it by his daily habits, is able to entertain his friends with a power impossible in strange quarters, or amid the artificial creations of asceticism. It is sufficient to say that the power is used—the result must be imagined.

More may be said about the entertainments residents provide in the large common rooms for larger parties. The one thing necessary is that the guests come by personal invitation—not as hungry people who need to be fed, or as members of a society who need to be bribed.

No one can live an active life without making acquaintances. A resident in a settlement will have already many friends—some made at school or college, some made in the course of his own daily business. He will add to those friends as he takes up duties in his new neighbourhood. He, as a school manager, will learn to know other managers ; he will be in frequent touch with the teachers, and, if he does his work well, will soon be on familiar terms with many of his parents.. As a guardian or vestryman, he will frequently meet neighbours who sit on the same board, he will come into contact with officials—nurses, clerks, inspectors,—and he will certainly have dealings with electors, who will praise or condemn his policy on the board.

As a member of a club he, by conversation, by joining in games, by taking part in the management, will soon enlarge the circle of his acquaintance, and number perhaps among his intimates, trade-unionists, friendly-society men, or co-operators. He will be interested in their interests, and will put his knowledge at their service.

As a leader of a reading party, he will every week meet those who are giving up time to tread the paths he has trod. He will find them anxious to know him, and willing to fall in with plans to visit places of interest in the country, or to travel abroad. He will make acquaintance with their friends, and will soon have quite a large visiting list.

A resident will thus have no difficulty in getting guests by personal invitation. He by arrangement with the other residents, will secure for the evening the use of the rooms he requires—drawing-room, dining-room, or lecture hall. He settles, let us say, on a drawing-room party of a hundred guests. He carefully selects them so that they will mix well and get interest in one another's talk. He takes special care to invite those who will help to bring about the mixing and get over the shyness which at first chills a party meeting in a room furnished "grandly." He himself receives each guest, and soon sets tea or refreshment going. Then, by the help of music, or by means of pictures, conversation starts. Little groups are formed, common subjects of interest are thrown amid the groups, and the chance is that the buzz of talk will proclaim the common pleasure.

But, perhaps, he settles on another sort of party. He will have a supper of thirty or seventy guests, and he invites the members of a society or of a club with which he is connected. Again he carefully chooses friends to meet the guests who will get and give enjoyment. He has the tables daintily spread and decorated with flowers, and he provides that the food shall be simple and abundant. Again he himself, in the drawing-room, receives each guest as he arrives, and, about half an hour after the time, conducts them all to the dining-room. At first the appearance of the room will cause a sort of awe to fall on the party, not an unpleasant awe, but one which yields to the influence of good food and good company. As supper ends there will be two or three short speeches, and then the whole party will adjourn to the drawing-room, to smoke, to sing songs, to tell tales until they part at twelve o'clock, conscious that the world is larger than it seemed and full of good fellows.

Or, to instance one more party, a resident determines to introduce some of his new friends to an old friend. He invites six or twelve to meet him on a Sunday or a Saturday afternoon. They start together, and get by train into the country. Then they walk to his old friend's house, which is, perhaps, three or four miles distant, and where there is a garden. Here they are welcomed and here, refreshed by food, by talk, by the sight of another sort of home life, they spend a pleasant time till they have to leave to catch a train for London.

Such is the hospitality possible in a settlement. It has at any rate more of the personal character than that provided by societies or officials. The host receives guests whom he knows, he receives them in his own home, and, amid the surroundings which express his tastes and his character, he gives himself as well as food and amusement. His hospitality is as true as any hospitality. He invites the pleasure of his guests' company, and the guests depart conscious that he has broken his host's bread and entered the circle of his friends.

If now the question be asked : What is the result of such hospitality? Is there any increase of good will between rich and poor? Do the meetings bring together the rich nation and the poor nation? Are they checking the horizontal cleavage of society? the answer must be that settlements are too few to have much visible result of any part of their efforts. It is remarkable that they should be so few, remarkable that men should recognize the needs and the power of the industrial classes, remarkable that they should be willing to do so much which seems hard, and yet refuse to make the sacrifice of giving up residence in a fashionable quarter. The attractions of society cannot be so overwhelming; it must be that men's imagination fails to grasp the use of residence among the poor, and that they go on living in the

F

old way because the new way seems fanciful. Until, however, the practice becomes more common it is impossible to collect results, to judge the gain which comes of knowledge, or to measure the power of friendship to harmonize conflicting interests. If settlements became so frequent as to cease to seem settlements, if they kept clear of all appearance of a mission, then rich and poor would so know one another that legislation and government would be armed to do the greatest good in the best way ; then people of different pursuits and with different incomes might, by equal manners and equal tastes, form the friendships which would hold them together in good times and in bad times.

But with regard to the hospitality of settlements it may, I think, be said that parties have promoted good will and given a bond which holds in its embrace many who were far apart. Hospitality has tended to that "cultivation of social life and manners " which, as Matthew Arnold says, "is equal to a moral impulse, for it works to the same end. . . . It brings them together, and makes them feel the need of one another."

THE UNIVERSITY SETTLEMENT

IN RELATION TO

LOCAL ADMINISTRATION

BY

PERCY ALDEN

WARDEN OF MANSFIELD HOUSE, CANNING TOWN

THE UNIVERSITY SETTLEMENT IN RELATION TO LOCAL ADMINISTRATION.

"Cannot the principle of self-interest destroy as well as found society? Yes ; self-interest must be followed by self-sacrifice or society will dissolve. Through the principle of self-interest society comes into being : through its annihilation it will endure."—ARNOLD TOYNBEE, *Industrial Revolution.*

THE question of the relation which the University Settlement should have to, and the part it should play in, the district in which it is situated is a somewhat perplexing one. It is a moot point as to how far the residents at the settlement are justified in taking any part in local administration. Some have gone so far as to say that such a course is an extremely dangerous one, and likely to lead to complications which will injure, not merely the settlement itself, but the efforts of social reformers in the locality. This criticism, however, is mostly extraneous, and seldom comes from men who are actually or actively engaged in social work, whether it be in East or South London, or in the poorer districts of any of our great cities.

It is often urged that social questions pure and

simple do not exist, that they cannot be dissociated from party politics, and that the efforts of the settlements to promote social reforms almost inevitably take on the air of partisanship. Our reply is, that such argument proves conclusively the importance of attempting to dissever and dissociate the two ideas, and that can only be done by urging good men with disinterested motives to enter the arena of conflict, and prove that there is a sphere of "pure politics" in which men of this type can engage.

The University Settlement ought, and frequently does, play a large part in educating the civic conscience, in forming and crystallizing public opinion on various social reforms. We suffer very much from the huge size of London, and the distance which separates the rich from the poor. It is almost as painful a symptom of the disease which afflicts the body politic, to find all the men of wealth and leisure living together on one side of London, as it is to find all the poor overworked or out-of-works massed and concentrated on the other. It would be better for London if these two sections of society could be brought into contact. It would do the rich man good to feel his responsibility for the condition of things which we find East and South, and the poor would respond to the brotherly spirit that is now overlaid and hidden by wealth and luxury.

It is impossible to value too highly the presence, in any working-class district, of men with some amount of leisure time and education who are willing to take a part in the public life of the locality. This, of course, applies especially to school-board work, but it has a bearing upon the Poor-Law and municipal work in general. One wealthy man who was willing to spend and be spent in the service of the people of East London, willing to wait until their very natural prejudice against him was overcome, might completely change the environment and life of the district in which he settled. If he stood as candidate for some public body, he would need to be careful at first lest it should be thought that he was attempting to supplant the labour representative. The workers are quick to detect and decry all attempts to use public bodies for selfish purposes. They have been over and over again deceived, sold to the highest bidder by those whom they trusted, and it is by no means to be wondered at that they regard with suspicion and jealousy any man from the outside who comes down to their district and asks them for a position of responsibility and trust ; but if such a man is willing to wait and work and prove to them that he seeks not his own interests or emolument— that, so far from seeking to aggrandize his own position, he is only desirous of bettering the position of the people whom he is professing to help—he will assuredly find them in the end supporting and assisting him in his effort to institute reforms and do away with abuses. He should be content with the privilege of serving, and should not allow that service to become merely the means to his own betterment.

To-day the working man is crying out for labour representation, and he should have it, and the more of it the better, provided that it be good ; but he will make a great mistake if, in his desire to have men who are pledged to carry out a labour policy, he refuses all other men who not only approve of the policy but also can give more time to carry it into effect. In fact, the only way to overcome the distrust which working men have of those who come from the middle and, to use a common expression, the upper classes is to show them by disinterested hard work that such suspicion and distrust are not always justified. It is much to be desiderated that the good feeling already existing between the settlements and the districts in which they are situated should be nourished and strengthened ; for, after all, the man who leaves Oxford or Cambridge to live in the East End is less likely to seek a position upon a public board from impure motives than many who sometimes offer themselves for election.

We occupy in England a very enviable position in this respect compared with the American Settlements, situated in towns like New York, Boston, Chicago, and Philadelphia. So far from obtaining direct representation on the various governing bodies, the residents at these foci of social life can only exercise, owing to the widespread municipal corruption, a very slight direct influence upon civic polity. I remember being told, at one settlement in the States, an amusing story which illustrates my point. A certain alderman had been supported by the settlement, not because he was an ideal candidate or suspected of being impeccable, but simply because it was considered that he would do less harm than his opponent. He was returned after a fierce struggle and, after his return, he coolly asked the chief organizer of the canvass what office or position he would give him as a reward. In this case I was informed that, to have run a "settlement" candidate who had no ulterior motives and no wish beyond that of being instrumental in effecting reforms, would have been to court certain failure.

Here in England it is often more a choice between fairly good candidates than absolutely bad, and perhaps the main thing is to secure the election of men who have just and righteous principles, no matter to what class or section of society they belong. It is infinitely to be preferred that the progress of social reforms should be gradual, even slow, than that public opinion should be retarded in growth for many years by one flagrant instance of corruption.

There are always some points in which the University man can be of special service upon a public body, provided that he be possessed of a fair amount of practicality and common sense. His range of ideas gives him a truer perspective ; his horizon is not so limited in extent; and, even when he is not a strenuous supporter of the labour movement, he often gives most valuable help where least expected. The thousand and one things that enter into all questions of sanitary reform, good houses, pure water, fresh air, free libraries, and so on, require not only men of experience, in so far as the workmen's needs are concerned, but also men of ideas who can initiate, and who can lay down lines upon which any given movement should proceed. The late Professor T. H. Green was a notable illustration of my meaning. There, in Oxford, was a man, a Professor of Moral and Metaphysical philosophy, with a mind so deep and profound that it has left its imprint upon Oxford teaching and upon Oxford schools, yet, with all his learning, he was one of the most practical and progressive reformers in the city council. Knowing the municipal history of Oxford of that time, and knowing many who shared with him civic responsibility, I can confidently affirm that Green's death left a great blank in the council, and that even to-day he is missed by many who knew his worth and had felt the force of his sterling and robust character.

What Green did in Oxford owing to his public spirit, disinterested motives, and untiring industry, University men, in a lesser degree perhaps, could do in every poor district. Persistent effort should be made to induce the working classes to put forward candidates of their own who can be trusted, and who are intelligent, and the University Settlements should encourage such candidature ; but while a sound public opinion in that direction, which takes a long time to create, is being formed, a man of university education, if he be thoroughly progressive, will do good service.

Toynbee Hall, Oxford House, Mansfield House, and the Bermondsey Settlement have all, in some measure, taken part in public life. Toynbee Hall has placed two members on the London School Board, of different opinions so far as politics go, yet both have done good work in their own separate departments, and both have displayed untiring zeal. Oxford House has usually several of its residents acting as school-

board managers : amongst them is the Head of the
House, who takes a great interest in the education
of children. Just lately it has returned a member
to the London School Board. In addition to
this, Mr. Bailward, who is connected with the House,
is upon the Board of Guardians. The Bermondsey
Settlement is represented on the Board of Guardians
by its Warden, and by the Head of the Women's
Department. Mansfield House claims, as its representatives, the Warden as a member of the Council
of West Ham; two of its executive committee as
members of the School Board ; and Miss Cheetham
as a member of the Board of Guardians, in addition
to board-school managers.

It is not, of course, absolutely necessary that
residents should be members of public bodies to
exercise a very effective influence on local administration. It is quite possible to call the attention of the
authorities to evils that should be remedied, and
arouse strong public opinion when they are overlooked ; but it is much more difficult to be sure of
success working on these lines alone, and the labour
is certainly much greater.

MUNICIPAL WORK.

The first thing that any one who wishes to take
part in local administration, whether in East London
or elsewhere, should aim at, is a thorough knowledge
of the social conditions under which the people of his
district live. Apart from this, successful action is

impossible. Just as you cannot legislate for a community unless you know its requirements and desires, so you cannot administer the law without familiarity with all that goes to make up the life of the citizens. To give one illustration : a man who is on the public health committee of some council or vestry should have, if he be in London, not only a knowledge of the locality in which he works and a personal acquaintance with the homes of its inhabitants, but also be versed in the working of the Public Health Amendment Act (London), 1891. If his work lie outside London, he should be acquainted with the Public Health Acts (1875), which apply to the whole of the country. And in both cases he will be called upon to administer the Housing of the Working Classes Act of 1890.

It is inevitable in poor districts that unsanitary conditions will prevail with regard to houses of the working classes unless drastic measures are taken to keep the landlord up to the mark, and to prevent the speculating and jerry builder having it all his own way. Landlords of the poorer districts are often not of the best type. I could cite many cases within my own experience where a landlord has summarily ejected a tenant from a house for no other reason than that the said tenant has, through our action, caused some scandalously insanitary condition of things in the house to be remedied. As often as not one finds that property has been farmed out by some other landlord, who wishes to be quit of the responsibility ; or the whole business is handed over to an agent, who works on commission for the absentee owner. The agent's one idea is to get the rent and to do as little as possible in the way of repairs.

Sometimes houses become insanitary because they have not been properly built in the first place. A large percentage of the houses in Canning Town, for example, which I know best, are really unfit for habitation owing to their dampness. In many cases they ought never to have been built, the land being marsh land and below the river level ; but as it was impossible to prevent that, owing to the egregious folly of a committee of the House of Commons, all the more care should have been taken to see that the foundations were good and the work thorough and solid. The University man obviously knows very little of building, but if he keep a watchful eye upon the officials and the inspectors he will generally find a corresponding alertness on their part. When they are corrupt, whether they be sanitary or building inspectors, he must move heaven and earth to get them dismissed. These men, like Cæsar's wife, should be above suspicion.

But while the University man seldom has a practical knowledge of building or road-making (unless we except the men who assisted Ruskin in his famous experiment at Oxford), he very frequently is the very person to assist in administering the Free Libraries Act. He knows the value of education, and usually he is able to get the Council or Vestry to adopt a much more generous educational policy than is common with these local bodies. Just because he is not altogether accustomed to East End life, he sees more clearly than the average man who has lived all his days in the district the value of public parks and bands, recreation grounds, and open spaces. He believes that baths and washhouses have a distinct moral value; that the planting of trees, with the provision of seats for the aged and tired—in fine, everything that brightens, lifts, and quickens the life of the people, is of great importance. Gradually he gets even those members to see with him who have been accustomed to judge each new venture by the amount of profit that it will yield, instead of considering the health, comfort, and happiness of the people. He has no objection to the municipalization of everything that can be profitably and safely undertaken. Indeed, Glasgow and the London County Council, etc., have proved that municipal bodies do well to build their own houses and public buildings, construct their own drains and sewers, run their own trams, gasworks, waterworks, lodging-houses. The average contractor or builder has a very natural objection to a council doing its own work; but it is just in proportion that this policy is supported that the end desired by the settlement is achieved. Public control over everything that concerns the well-being of the people is daily becoming more and more an assured fact, and the settlement welcomes the development, for it means an enlightened public spirit.

School Board.

The work of the School Board is par excellence the sphere of activity for the University Settler, whether as member of the Board itself or as a local manager.

All over East and South London these "lighthouses of the future," as Sherlock Holmes has called the Board schools, tower above the surrounding blocks of dwelling-houses. Nothing could be more important than to have capable and intelligent representatives on the School Board ; for upon the proper education of the children depends largely the welfare of the future democracy. It is one of "Life's little Ironies," as Thomas Hardy would say, that the very districts which need most money for the education of their children have least of it ; and the same thing applies to the men who represent the educational interests of the people. It is true that, at an election, there is no lack of candidates ; but these too frequently come forward from far other desires and with far other qualifications than can be described as educational. There are men who wish to get on the Board merely for the honour the position confers. Others serve merely party interests ; for example, the "distressed ratepayer" party. It is their business to stop every possible expense, regardless of the fact that the same policy in bygone years is making them pay heavily in the present day. Surely it is better to spend money in giving a child a good education during its school life, at a cost of about £3 per annum, than to provide him with board and lodging in strict seclusion afterwards at a cost of £24 or £40 per annum, according to the nature of his retirement. It is an excellent thing to have *bonâ fide* working men on the board, to see that, in the erection of buildings and other works, fair and honest conditions of labour are enforced. It is good to have experienced business

men who can handle the finances and examine work
done, with a critical eye. It is good that, while
theological controversies rage, the denominations
should be fairly balanced. But it becomes all the more
imperative that, in the composition of a Board, there
should be some at least who will act as educationists
pure and simple, emphasizing its primary function.
This the University man is fitted to do. He has
received himself a fair education as educations go ;
he believes in the "ladder of learning" from the
Elementary school up to the University itself;
he is freed as a rule from local, theological, and party
bias ; and if he will only remember that Elementary
education is not University education, and that to be
educated and to educate are two very different things,
he may be of incalculable service on the Board.
Further, he probably has more time to give to committee work than the busy tradesman and shopkeeper,
and, after all, the great work of a School Board is
done in committee, and not on board night. It is in
the various committees that one gathers up all the
complex threads and details of school life, familiarity
with which is indispensable in educational work.

These remarks will apply with almost equal
weight to the school manager. Who shall overrate
the value of a good manager? He deserves higher
praise than Solomon bestows upon the good wife.
And University Settlement residents are some of
the most useful managers in East London. They
visit the schools regularly and frequently. They see
that the body as well as the mind is trained and fed ;
and though, perhaps, Plato's ideal of μυνσικη και

γυμναστικη is, like his ideal State, difficult of attainment, it is something which they aim at and in part achieve.

Poor Law.

And now as to work upon Boards of Guardians. Here, if anywhere, you need men who are not only experienced in separating evil from good, the sheep from the goats, but who have in addition high ideals. The guardian should be able to make the very best of those who come before him for relief, treating each case on its own individual merits. If there is one thing that the poor-law needs just now, it is to be lifted out of the dull formal routine of red tape into which, in too many cases, its administration has fallen. It is not improbable that the most radical and sweeping changes will come by way of poor-law administration, *e.g.* in the treatment of the *unemployed*. The tax upon a guardian who wishes to do his duty is very heavy now. It will be heavier in the future. Every year the work will grow and become more wide-reaching in its scope, and (*pace* some members of the Charity Organization Society) various fresh departures and reforms are to be expected and desired. The questions of farm colonies for the unemployed, the establishment of cottage homes for pauper children, the classification of paupers, the improvement of the conditions of the aged poor, and, in relation to this, old-age pensions,—these things and an immense variety of smaller matters all cry out for earnest and careful consideration.

But, it may be asked, "All this merely affects the

G

man who is on some local body ; how does it touch the man whose stay in East London, or in the poorer parts of any of our great cities, is too short to allow of his election on any such body?" For them there is a sphere of work not perhaps so clearly marked out and defined, but none the less important and valuable. We have referred to the school-board manager. Would it not be possible to do the same work with regard to public health that the manager does for education. The Rev. Canon Barnett has shown in Whitechapel how men like Edward Denison, Arnold Toynbee, and a large number of men of a later generation can be of the utmost use in assisting the local public bodies and keeping an eye upon their movements. There are few places where a properly organized committee of working men, with a Settlement Resident acting as secretary, could not materially assist the Medical Officer and sanitary inspectors for the district. This has been done not unsuccessfully in connection with the Brotherhood Society at Mansfield House.

Then, again, there are Boards of Guardians in London that could in some way or other be materially helped and strengthened from outside. The relieving officers are mostly overworked men, and there are often special cases which are inadequately treated, simply because the officer cannot possibly give all the time necessary for full inquiry. Without hesitation, I say again, it is the bounden duty of the residents at a University Settlement, not merely to take a superficial interest in all the transactions of the various public bodies, but also, by personal acquaintance with their local officials, to add their quota of labour in the administration of civic affairs. There is a very great deal of truth in W. T. Stead's idea of a civic Church. The religious aspect of civic duty in regard to "this mountainous mass of postponed problems" is apt to be overlooked, even by those men who are professedly religious. It is quite possible that the most important reforms in our industrial life will come by way of the Council and the Board of Guardians; and even supposing it were not so, and your House of Commons were on the *qui vive* for every new and promising measure of legislation, what would it all amount to apart from capacity to administer the law when made?

My feeling is that local bodies will lead the way in the solution of our social problems, provided that we supply good enough men. The time is ripe for all sorts of valuable experiments. We may miss the path and make mistakes, but we can see at any rate some distance ahead. There is a great call for men who will face the problems of casual labour and the unemployed, either by acting on the council or acting with it.

Councils, Vestries, and Boards of Guardians are crying out for some plan by which the honest unemployed may be relieved. They are not always anxious to do anything although they cry; but when they are, they not seldom seem at a loss what to do. Charles Booth and others like him have given us ground upon which to go. We have a large number of facts, figures, and statistics. Sometimes we are overawed and weighted down by them; but it is not enough to know that so many thousands of men apply daily for work at the dock gates and fail to get it, or that there are tens of thousands of men in London out of employment, men who would be willing to work and who would do it well—men, on the other hand, who are being demoralized, degraded, and dispirited by the lack of it. We must *do* something. What can we do?

For one thing, we can attempt to perfect whatever schemes of relief work are already in operation. Where no scheme is in operation, we can see to it that whatever is started, is started on right lines, or at any rate we can use the influence we possess in this direction. All of us recognize that relief work at present is a sort of necessary evil, and that what will have to come sooner or later is the entire reorganization of labour on a more ethical basis.

Meanwhile the University man can, to some extent, atone for deficiency in method by the enthusiasm of his own personal interest. His aim should be, while relieving the present necessities of the unemployed, to make the scheme subserve the real end in view, and supply data for the reformer that is to be. Opportunities will not be wanting in the immediate future. It is a foregone conclusion, I wish it were not, that every winter will see, for years to come, a recurrence of the poverty epidemic, partly due, of course, to vice and intemperance, a sort of permanent yearly factor, but largely due to the growing uncertainty and lack of employment.

The "citizen-student," as the resident at the University Settlement has been called, may very well devote himself to helping forward the solution of some part of this great problem. The industrial struggle, though it has passed out of its cruder stages, inevitably means to-day that a large portion of those we are accustomed to call "unfit" are rendered still more unfit by the intensity of the competition. The poverty which results from casual labour and the lack of employment has become a national disease. From one point of view it is a national crime, and, as such, must be atoned for by long years of ceaseless effort to effect the necessary reforms in our existing social system. And if we are told that local and imperial legislation for these objects is paternal government, and ought not to be resorted to in the nineteenth century, let us answer, in the words of Sir Arthur Helps, "Never is paternal government so needful as when civilization is most advanced." Here we are crowded together in a place that is "treeless, colourless, bathless, mudful, smoke-stained, its amusements coarse, the dress of its inhabitants hideous, its food adulterated, its drink pernicious," and, we may add, its houses insanitary. Poverty, as Stopford Brooke says, is not merely lack of food or clothes, but "that condition of things in which, for lack of means, no true development of the natural powers of any man or woman can be reached." Using the word in this very true sense, there are hundreds of thousands of men and women in England who, just because they are ignorant and apathetic about these necessaries of a higher life, must be raised to see their importance and assisted in the obtaining of them. Their environment tends to corrupt and

demoralize, making the work of succeeding generations far harder and more difficult. At present we
are expecting an evil tree to produce good fruit, un-
tilled and untended land to produce a rich harvest.
If this is the soil in which the future generation has
to grow and develop, will it develop or degenerate?
That is the question we have to answer, and, having
answered it in the only way possible, let the resident
at the University Settlement continue to take an
interest even in the petty details of local administration, or the unattractive person of the casual labourer;
for, as Wordsworth says,—

> "He who feels contempt
> For any living thing, hath faculties
> Which he has never used; that thought with him
> Is in its infancy."

THE CHILDREN'S COUNTRY HOLIDAYS FUND AND THE SETTLEMENTS

BY

CYRIL JACKSON

TOYNBEE HALL

THE CHILDREN'S COUNTRY HOLI-DAYS FUND, AND THE SETTLE-MENTS.

PROBABLY the first thing that appeals to the University Settler is the difficulty of getting enough fresh air and exercise in London. At the Universities, men and women have aimed at the *mens sana in corpore sano*, and they come down to the gloomy cramped streets of London to feel the want of space themselves, and to see all round them the children growing up under conditions which make healthy growth of body almost impossible. The foul air of their crowded rooms is exchanged for the sooty air outside. There is no place for free exercise. The school playgrounds are all too small, and there is nothing left for the youngsters but the street. A pitiable playground, indeed! Does not our University cricketer yearn for a bit of grass for the youngsters who play cricket with such spirit, with their coats piled up to form the wicket, on the hot pavement or the stones of the streets, which are not rolled smooth before the match? What a haven of rest is the country to the quieter mortals! and what a splendid playing-place for the energetic, where you can hit a ball as hard as you like without fear of the stick from an irate neighbour whose window was too close to the batsman!

It is not surprising, therefore, that the work of sending ailing children into the country for a fortnight's holiday has been warmly taken up by the University Settlements.

It is very suitable for men or women who are anxious to devote some time to their poorer neighbours. It especially appeals to those of us who are not too old to sympathize with the keen enjoyment of the children in their stay in the country village. There they will make new friends and get free space for games. They can watch birds and beasts, pluck flowers, or catch butterflies; there, too, they will get renewed health and the buoyant spirits which come from fresh air and change of scene. The University Settler has come to live among his poorer neighbours, to share their life as far as possible and learn their thoughts. He will see around him all the larger sides of social life, local government of Vestry and Poor Law, trade-unions working to raise wages, friendly societies helping the sick, charitable effort expended in various ways, usefully or harmfully. He wants to help, even if he cannot yet hope to guide. The children are apparently the easiest and most hopeful to deal with. The need of change of air is one of their most obvious wants. The first impulse is probably to pick out some poor children from those around, and to send them off, free of charge, to a home. But this soon appears inadequate and unmethodical, and experience shows the greater advantages of thorough work and the advisability of recognizing that eventually the rich can never do things for the poor, but can merely make it easier for them to do things for themselves.

Experience will show the danger of free funds, and the danger of overlapping where there are many little funds not working in harmony.

The settlements have wisely fallen in with the general scheme—uniting themselves with so well-known a university man as the Hon. Alfred Lyttelton. Besides the general benefits of co-operation, the residents, being a changing body in each settlement, have recognized the advantage of joining existing institutions instead of starting fresh responsibilities.

The size of the society in itself guarantees more careful work. The experience of all is at the service of each, and the traditions of past labours are especially valuable to men just down from the different world of the universities. The large society can afford an inspector of country homes; can relieve its local volunteers of much of the worry of money-getting; can furnish printed matter—forms and papers—at cheaper cost; and, finally, can always be grumbled at if anything goes wrong. Its size would be weakness if it were over-centralized, but each of the 50 local committees has a vigorous individual life, and in 1894 the efforts of their 500 members enabled over 28,000 children to get not less than a fortnight's change.

The children are boarded in cottages, in villages within about eighty miles of London, under the supervision of some responsible country neighbour. To find the right people for this supervision many country friends are needed. The settlements have been particularly fortunate in finding good homes, where the country correspondent has an interest in the children sent from their London acquaintances, resisting the temptation of pouring some of the £14,000 spent by the society each year in the villages into some poor cottage. It is better to find villages some distance from London, where the people are less in touch with London and will take more interest in their guests. The interchange between town and country is of real value, and the turning back ever so slightly of the stream of immigration from country to town is of some use to our villages.

The ideal country visitor knows every cottager—has seen all the offered accommodation, and, besides this, looks after the children when they have arrived. Fortunately there are many hundreds who take this living interest in the children under their care, who help them to enjoy themselves, and who have taken pains to place them with respectable and kindly people. It is very seldom that there is any complaint of the neglect of the little ones.

The London work is by no means easy. A classical education is certainly not the only equipment needed. The good Country Holidays Fund visitor needs judgment, tact, and experience of the poor. All work which implies investigation requires previous knowledge of the surrounding circumstances. The new visitor should, perhaps, at first confine himself to revisiting old cases and collecting payments until he has learned the general lines of the work.

The selection of the children is the initial

difficulty. The society works through the day schools, for there all the children of the elementary school class are enrolled. The members of the University Settlement start with a great advantage if they are already school managers. As such they may have helped with savings-banks or boot-clubs, and so seen the thrifty parents, or they may have helped to investigate the cases recommended for free dinners, and in this way have gained a knowledge of the circumstances of some of the most destitute families.

As residents in a settlement they have very likely served in this capacity, or have been almoners of the society for the relief of distress, or members of the local Charity Organization Committee. Through these agencies they can take up the poorest cases, and give them not only the means of change of air, but some more thorough help.

Whether with this experience or not the first step will be to interview the day-school teachers, and learn from them with the help of the attendance registers which are the most ailing children. They must learn, too, what the teachers can tell about the characteristics of the children selected.

Daily intercourse is certain to give knowledge of their natures, and indirectly some acquaintance with the character of their parents, just as it is the residence in their midst and daily opportunities of meeting which make the University Settler more able to deal with his neighbours than if he " came down " from the west. When the children begin to know him they will run up in the street when they meet

him, and though the conversation usually stops at
"Hullo," there are often, and could be oftener, little
confidences as to their own or their family affairs.
The children are much more expressive than their
parents, and will give valuable, because indirect and
unconscious, insight into the ways and lives of the
poor.

Of course, when this selection in the schools has
been made, the homes have to be visited, and the
parents invited to send their children away and to
contribute a fair share of the cost, which is about
thirteen shillings a head for the fortnight. This work
requires both skill and kindliness. It will be a great
help if the visitor is already known. If, for instance,
the child introduces him with "Mother, this is the
gentleman who comes to our school," a footing of
past friendliness and neighbourliness makes the
relation different at once. The teachers are very
excellent visitors themselves, if they have time to
give to it; but merely seeing the children and
occasionally the parents in the school does not give
much insight into the life of the family.

There is much to be done—the indifferent parents
must be made to see the benefit of the change, the
poor ones the possibility of putting by small sums
towards the expense. Many visits to the same mother
may be necessary, and to send the very poor children
who are generally those with careless and slovenly
parents, many a chat is needed before the mother
rises to the occasion. Not infrequently, too, the re-
solve, when formed, is not strong enough to bear fruit
without further visits. To send one of the very poor

children requires more labour than a dozen of the artisan class.

It is true that many of the poorest class go hopping and fruit-picking, and get a long change of air in this way. Those that do not go are the standing problem of the visitor. It is not the payment which stands in the way, but difficulties in providing clothes or getting the children clean. A clothes-lending depôt has worked well, and some committees have arranged for baths and cutting of hair.

Great tact is wanted in arriving at a just estimate of the parents' resources. The visitor who takes with him his printed form and asks a string of questions too often hurts the feelings of the parents, or else tempts them to depreciate their incomes and exaggerate their difficulties. The formal question brings a deceitful answer from those who have no good feeling, and drives those who have the pride of respectability into the silence of offended dignity— they hate what they consider inquisitiveness. The visitor who chats about home circumstances and the baby, the high rents and irregularity of work, and shows an interest in these things,—who points out the cost of the child in the country, and the need that each should contribute what they can afford, so that more children can go—will generally get all the necessary information pleasantly and readily, and be able to correct at once any little misstatement of income, and elicit a cheerful promise of a good payment.

Parents like the compliment that is paid them

when they are invited to give more to help their poorer neighbours. The minimum to be obtained from each must be fixed by equity, the maximum by their self-respect and generosity. In this work, again, residence is of the greatest value. If the visitor knows the father in the men's club, or the elder brothers in boys' clubs or evening classes, there is at once a tie of friendship and a means of estimating wages.

Elder brothers can be induced to take an interest in their youngsters. There was at least one case this year where two elder club lads volunteered to pay each for a little brother, while the widowed mother sent the little girl. This is the right spirit of self-help and family affection, which can often be evoked by a friend's suggestion. Parents are too apt to ignore their elder wage-earning children—they receive so much a week from them, they assume they cost that amount at home, and they neither count this contribution in the family earnings when they are stating the latter to the visitor, nor do they think of any possibility of response to a further appeal to them for an additional sum for the special object of the little one's health.

The visitor should always strive to maintain independence and evoke self-help. Eventually the Country Holidays Fund may consist of parents' contributions, and the committees would provide the means of the holiday, and not its cost. The Londoner has no means of finding good country homes, and co-operation secures cheap fares and effective supervision, but the London parent who gets these from the society must eventually feel that the cost of his child's keep and fare is his own business.

Experience shows the sad fact that nearly one-third of the children originally selected in the schools do not, after all, go for their fortnight's change. The reasons are various, but when the school visitor knows roughly what amount of the local fund is allotted to his particular school he will be able to estimate the numbers which can be sent, and then devote all his pains to seeing that those who most need the holiday really get it. When the parents' interest has been thoroughly aroused they will make an effort to find the money. Where they cannot be expected to part with a lump sum, arrangements can generally be made to collect their contributions before-hand in weekly instalments. In this the school teachers are generally most kind and helpful. If there is not already a school bank, they are most ready to help in receiving the children's pence and entering them on their cards, even if the collection is begun at the very beginning of the year, months before the holiday. When the parents have once paid a substantial sum the children very seldom fail to get their holiday.

Perhaps the most wearisome part of the whole work is the committee meeting, when the cases that have been selected and inquired into by each visitor have to be submitted to the judgment of the whole body. Long and tiring as these meetings are, they are necessary. In this way alone is uniformity of action preserved and involuntary favouritism checked. In some districts all the visitors are members of the committee, in others a smaller executive body is appointed, which goes through the cases as each visitor brings them up. Whichever method is adopted it is well to introduce fresh elements if possible—men and women of experience of the district, who may not have time to visit, but have knowledge and the judicial faculty. The small executive, for instance, would be admirable if composed of five or six members, including one of the oldest of the clergy or a head deaconess, some representative of the Charity Organization Society, and some one who was a member of or in close touch with trade or benefit societies. Representatives of all denominations and the various social efforts should be invited to co-operate. A layman, or lady, is often better able to unite the different charitable agencies, and the University Settlement should have people well qualified to act in this direction.

Some of the residents in University Settlements would always be interested in working men's societies—would be members of the Foresters or Oddfellows, or in some neighbourly way would know the working-class leaders. If some good working men or women can themselves be secured on the committees there will be great gain. The society would be the better for some more direct representatives of the class it benefits. The settlements ought to be able to find such men among their club or trade-society friends. But, failing this, some resident who has been devoting himself to trade problems, and has been examining the questions of wages and fluctuations of work, would be of the greatest assistance on the committee although he might be unable to take up a school or visit homes.

In raising some local funds, too, the help of these men would be invaluable. Every district ought to try and send money into the central office, not only to relieve the central committee of a share of the labour of money-getting, but also because it is right that the locality should have the opportunity and feel the responsibility of helping its own children. The amounts now raised are small.

This year the fifty local committees, including the richest parts of London as well as the poorest, only sent in about £1500 out of a total of nearly £12,000. There was, however, an interesting contribution obtained through the Phœnix Society branches in Bethnal Green, who were interested in the Fund by the residents of Oxford House.

The committee has, however, to spend most of its time in passing cases.

The visitor has seen the child's home, obtained particulars, and formed an estimate of the circumstances of the parents, but some one on the committee may have had a longer and wider knowledge; fresh facts are brought out—perhaps a new complexion put on the whole case. Then, too, the less-experienced visitor gets an insight into the operations of the older members. But the main help of the committee to the too good-natured visitor is that it is a convenient abstraction by reference to which a friendly coercion may be brought to bear on the unwilling parent who is trying to shirk a fair payment. It is not nearly so difficult to get a higher offer when the visitor can fall back on the committee's orders, and many a visitor in bringing forward his or her case, says, " They say they can only pay so much, but I hope you will put it up, as I am sure they can pay more." The working man on the committee, or the neighbour who lives among them, and knows the rate of wages and amount of work available at the time, makes short work of these shirkers, having a righteous sense of the fair and equal.

It is a great pity that the country holiday committees die down in the winter. There would be some work for them always in keeping in touch with parents and children, and there must also actually be many children needing change all the year round.

But for the bulk of the children who need change, without being definitely ill, it is far preferable that they should go away during the school holidays, in order that they may not lose their education. Every child absent from school is not only losing its own chances of learning, but is making the task of the teacher more difficult, and, by necessitating constant repetition of the class-work, is hindering its more regular fellows of their proper progress, and tending to dull them. There is so much less holiday, too, to be spent in the streets, which are not the best holiday playground, with their noise and drunkenness, their foul air and dangerous traffic. Difficult as it is to find enough country homes to send the whole number of the Fund's beneficiaries away in a couple of batches, this must be aimed at.

In the country it is essential that the reception of children should not become a trade to be carried on as long as possible during the summer months. We must try and insure that the cottagers shall feel it a labour of love. This is possible for a few children.

Two pairs of little Londoners are interesting. They have different ways which it is amusing to compare. Their London ignorance and their London quickness are pleasant to see and hear. But when fresh ones continue to arrive the personal interest must begin to flag, and the comparisons made will not be between Tom's oddities and Jack's quaint stories, but between the trouble given by the one batch compared with the quietness of the previous one.

But before we have got our children to the country the transit of all this human freight must be effected. The arrangements are made in the country, the correspondent there has seen the cottagers finally, and talked over all the various little difficulties. In London we must first inspect the children we are going to send, and we must consult the lists of the medical officer of health to see there is no danger of their taking infection with them.

The responsibility of importing fever or other disease into a village is no light one. The poorest children, too, must be carefully examined as to personal cleanliness. In this we must often again fall back on the knowledge and good nature of the teachers, who can persuade a mother that her girl's outwardly fine head of hair must be removed in the interests of health and cleanliness. Then on the fatal day the whole of the London stations swarm with little parties of children, ticketed and labelled by the careful worker, and with their excitement duly restrained. At last they are off, and there is a brief respite.

It is, however, a respite only, not an absolute cessation of responsibility, for it is very necessary that the London visitor should be within touch if anything goes wrong in the country, or, as is more frequently the case, if anything is supposed to be going wrong. A child writes home, and the mother fancies all sorts of things, which sometimes lead her to go down for her offspring, when a word with the visitor would have set all right. Or, as happened this year, a child writes that "there are thirteen of us at the Cross—it is a queer place." This is supposed at once to be a public-house of the worst character, and the imagination of a strong temperance advocate informs the neighbours of terrible doings— overcrowding and rowdiness. The Cross being really a quiet outlying hamlet.

To those who have had all the trouble and worry of arrangement, the best reward is to visit the children in the country. Their happiness is so obvious and genuine; they have so much to tell; they are so pleased to see a London friend and tell it. If the London visitor gets up the rules carefully, and is not shy of making a thorough inspection, he can be very useful in going over the cottages and seeing the sleeping accommodation. If he feels uncertain what to allow, and condones any irregularities from a feeling that the country correspondent knows best, rather than say anything disagreeable, his visit had better be to the children as a friend and not as an inspector.

Luckily, just grounds of complaint as to accommodation are very rare. The country people are, as a rule, thoroughly interested in the children, especially, of course, in the small centres, where very few are received at a time. On these few is focussed the whole kindliness of the village, and the fewer they are the less likely they are to alienate friendliness by mischievous pranks.

At one place one hears of rides in the grocer's cart or on the hay-waggon; at another there has been a local school treat or festival, and the little strangers have been included. Riding the donkey, feeding the fowls, attempting to milk the cow, helping in the haymaking, picking apples (with allowed subtractions),—all and every phase of ordinary country existence is delightful and new to the town-bred child. If their London friend comes down all these joys are recounted, while he, in return, may bring tales of the brother's or father's doings in the club.

Even if this country visit cannot be paid, the children can be met at the station on their return laden with flowers and vegetables. Later on, too, the brown faces can be seen in the class at school. The country holiday children are almost invariably bright spots there.

In seeing the children off, bringing them back, collecting their payments and the like, the merest novice can find easy and pleasant work. In nothing that we do among the poor is the benefit more immediately visible. The holiday is complete in itself. There is an obvious result of the trouble taken in the happier faces and stouter health of the children who have come back. How seldom can we see the result of our sowings! Too often the return is not yet, and we sometimes fancy it will never be.

There is a further word to be said. So far we have been considering rather how the University Settlement can help the Children's Country Holidays Fund, how the fact of neighbourhood enables the resident to enter more fully into the life of the people and so makes him more effective than any outside help. But the Country Holidays Fund ought also to help the settlement. It affords a splendid starting point for future work and future friendships. Perhaps the parents are more readily influenced through their children than in any other way. Those whom they see taking much pains and trouble for their children's happiness, earn their gratitude far more than those who bring them money. It is the sacrifice of ease they value; they can see the labour and appreciate it: every one among the poor assumes, however, that money is nothing to a University man. From this basis of a common work the parents feel a real friendship for the child's friend, and are ready to do anything possible in return. They begin to recognize that our aim in living among them is really that we may serve them; they begin to believe in our dis-interestedness—an idea, alas! which they are very slow to grasp. If, after the holiday, we can keep in touch with them, and keep this friendship alive, we shall be forming a band of helpers of our settlement

who will lead to the readier reception in the neighbourhood of any help, educational or otherwise, that is
offered. Such friendship is firm, because they have
learned to trust the visitor and respect him in the
discussion of all the little details and plans of the trip.
A chat over the best arrangements as to boots and
jerseys is a small thing at the time, but the sense of
the sharing of the work gives all the confidence and
friendliness of fellow-workers which can hardly be
obtained in any other way, and which may hereafter
be of great service to the progress of the work of the
settlement. Even the most indifferent have some
fondness for their children. The better class of
parents, who would be above ordinary relief and
would be too shy for ordinary conversation, may feel
the need of change for a child, and in this way come
into pleasant contact with the visitor, and, seeing him
a friend, find that the settlement is there to be used
by the working man. The mission, perhaps, of the
settlement in the Country Holidays Fund is to
introduce more of the spirit of neighbourly co-
operation, and more of the working-class feeling into
the work ; to bridge the gulf between donor and
recipient ; to make it the working man's own affair,
which he feels to be his own ; and to bring his common
sense and knowledge of his own class to the aid of
the Fund. The mission of the Country Holidays
Fund to the settlement is to give a ready outlet for
enthusiastic service of the poor, and to furnish a
means of getting their friendship, which must be
the chief means of enabling it to do effective service,

MAYFIELD HOUSE

(CHELTENHAM LADIES' COLLEGE SETTLEMENT)

BY THE HEAD,

MISS MAUD CORBETT

.

MAYFIELD HOUSE.

THIS settlement of ladies, which was started in the autumn of 1889, consists of committee, lady warden or head, and a collective guild, which is entirely composed of old Cheltenham College girls, no one being allowed to join the guild till she has left or is just leaving Cheltenham College. It now comprises eight hundred members. This guild having decided on supporting a settlement in Bethnal Green, obtained a lease of Mayfield House, but before it had entered on its occupation, proposals were made by a committee of Oxford and London ladies interested in Bethnal Green, to share for the present in the use and maintenance of the house, which proposal was agreed to.

The object of the settlement was to help forward work already existing and organized ; and to supply experience to those who need it, in wishing to undertake work elsewhere, and who may be glad to prepare themselves by a training of some months in a settlement such as this, which gives them an opportunity of seeing the many different branches of work carried on outside and apart from the house, and the means of judging the effect and practical results of such work, and whether it may be useful to them wherever their sphere in the future may be.

1. Help was at once given in various departments to the home arts and industries. On Tuesday and Thursday evenings some seventy or eighty boys might have been seen working at the following trades: Venetian or bent-iron work, leather work, brass work, English and Swiss wood-carving. The object of these classes was to give the boys some interest beyond the routine of their daily work. The greater number of them being in different factories, where days and weeks were spent in that monotonous work which is the necessary outcome of divided labour. Boys were not admitted to these classes before the age of sixteen.

2. The efforts of the residents at Mayfield House were diverted to the following objects, amongst others :—

Parish work in all its various branches, including district visiting, mother's meetings, Bible classes, Sunday school teaching, etc.

Choral classes in Mayfield House and at Poplar. The former composed the choir for week-day services during Advent and Lent in the Parish Church. The latter helped with the musical part in the lectures to working men, given on Sunday afternoons in the Mission Church at Poplar.

Help was given at penny dinners. These dinners were sold at a cheap rate to the very poor, during the winter months. Also in connection with this was started a dining-room for poor men at work in the neighbourhood, giving them a chance of obtaining a good dinner at the same low rate.

3. It was at the expressed wish of the wives of artisans that ambulance classes and nursing classes in Mayfield House were first originated, and the regular attendance at them showed they were fully appreciated.

Work in connection with the Charity Organization Society was taken up; as also work in connection with the society for befriending young servants, commonly known as the Mabys, and a club for factory girls twice a week. Sales of new and old clothes to the poor were occasionally held. The house was also used for Sunday classes, and a good many entertainments given there at Christmas time.

By degrees there came changes as to the branches of work undertaken or helped in. Owing to various circumstances, perhaps, it seemed better for one branch to be given up, the need for it might have gone, while pressing need might appear for another to be taken up. The I.C.A.A. (Invalid Children's Aid Association) was one of these. The aim of the society is to provide for each child a friend, who should undertake to give to it, as far as possible, personal service; also the special medical advice that may be necessary to the child, or admission into a suitable hospital; in fact, anything which love with common sense may suggest. And it is sometimes hoped that the work does not stop with the child, but that, it may be through a book lent, or the love and kindness shown to the child, a father or mother may have learned to believe in something good, and to look beyond their own troubles and burdens. In some homes the little invalid seems just the one spot of brightness, no scolding or threats fall to its share, but a softer look comes over the mother's face as she talks of it, or looks at it ; and this raises a hope that the little child is unconsciously God's instrument for good in the family. Though it must be confessed there is another side, when it is shown, only too plainly, that the poor child is felt to be a drag and a trouble, and so better out of the way.

In 1892 the Oxford ladies left Mayfield House, and formed their own settlement, under the name of St. Margaret's. Part of their work had been a girl's club (factory) attached to the house. This they took with them, but help is still given to the parish club once or twice a week.

And now we come to a very important branch of work undertaken at Mayfield House, namely, Board-school work—a resident being manager in one group of schools, making friends with the teachers, also with the parents of those children who attend seldom or never, getting them to take an interest in their children going regularly to school; sometimes raising the moral tone of the homes, and finding out the reason for bad attendances, which may prove to be simply indolence or want of care, sometimes want of clothes. In conjunction with Board schools, and Church voluntary schools belonging to the parish, the Children's Country Holidays Fund has been most successfully worked. Many parties meeting at May-field House, start off with various kind friends who take them across London to Euston, Paddington, or

some terminus, where they are placed under the care
of the guard, and all anxiety is over. Sometimes
there are many disappointments, such as when the
money is not paid up at the last minute, and the
child cannot go ; but, when all is successfully accomplished, the troubles and annoyances seem nothing
compared to the pleasure of having secured a fortnight's happiness and country air for the children.

Another very considerable part of the work at
Mayfield House is with pupil teachers of Board
schools, one worker being honorary secretary of a
centre to the London Pupil Teachers' Association.
The endeavour is to make the house as attractive as
possible : sometimes there is a social evening, which
means asking them to tea, followed by music and
recitations, in which they are often pleased to help ;
sometimes an invitation is sent out, saying the residents are "at home" at a certain hour. Every
Saturday various classes are held, such as artistic
embroidery, elocution, painting, singing, and chip-
carving. These classes must be in the form of recreation, though it is insisted, as far as possible, that
the pupil teachers shall regularly attend any class
which they may enter, and that the work shall be, of
its sort, thorough and good.

The lives of these girls, in many cases, must be
very lonely and very hard. The aim is to get them
to look upon the residents as their friends, and that
by simple, quiet, and, where possible, individual effort.
That this intercourse may not begin and end by being
merely social, it is hoped to form a Bible class on
Sundays. When the great number of pupil teachers

I

is taken into consideration, the power they must be in England in teaching and forming the ideas of the next generation, the immense influence for good or evil they must have, this effort cannot be too keenly made ; and ought, indeed, to be a very important part of the work of a settlement such as Mayfield House, which is formed by a college guild.

We have also joined a branch of the Women's Co-operative Guild. The branch dates its commence- ment from last spring ; it now consists of nearly forty members, almost all of whom are working women. We meet in Oxford Hall once a week, when we sometimes discuss the real meaning of co-operation, in contrast with individualism ; and how we can best help the society forward—whether by gaining recruits, by forwarding education, or by creating more social life among its members by realizing more we belong to a body, and cannot each act for self alone.

The people among whom we work are mostly of the better class—that is, not criminal. They work principally as cabinet-makers, boot-makers, labourers, matchbox and fancy-box makers, and brush-makers. There is great poverty, mostly owing to the de- pressed state of trade. You hear on all sides, " I would do anything, if only I could get it." They are not, as a rule, pauperized, but have an immense amount of self-respect and independence. Very patient and ever willing to help each other, very ready to be friendly, it is often quite touching to see the interest they take in us as their friends, eager to enter into our pleasures, and always hoping, as each departs for her holiday, that she will enjoy herself,

and come back very well ; not for an instant con-
trasting their own lives, where so many a poor mother
has to toil on from year's end to year's end, never
getting any rest or change from her labours—with the
exception of one day, perhaps, in the country during
the summer, when they do seem to throw off all
care, and behave like children, swinging, running
races, playing games with what appears an absolute
freedom from care, until the time comes when we
have to collect and say good-bye to the friends who
have been entertaining us so kindly ; then you hear on
all sides, "Dear, how quick the time has gone, to be
sure!" or, "I should like to have stayed all night."
They accept the inevitable, though, most cheerfully,
their tongues never flagging all the journey home.

In some cases the families are almost entirely
supported by the scanty earnings of the mothers and
elder children. The men are so soon looked upon as
too old, and therefore put on one side—there seems
so little thought or consideration for the individual.
And this, perhaps, strikes one as being one of the
saddest phases of life down here. It seems like
saying, "Get all you can out of a man : after that,
leave him ; trouble no more—his day is over." But
even to this there are bright exceptions.

Their aims and ideas of life and conduct may
not be high, but it is wonderful to notice how, as a
rule, they live up to their ideas. Still there is a great
mass of indifferentism to high aspirations and noble
standards of right and wrong ; there seems a dulness
—a want of power to look beyond their own daily
routine of cares and troubles, and the terrible anxiety

as to where the necessary food and clothing for the children is to come from, or how long they can keep a roof over their heads.

We workers often feel, though we may be striving to help them, to lift them to higher aspirations, nobler standards of right and wrong, how much we are learning from them, from their patient endurance, their cheerfulness, their thankfulness ; and, considering their surroundings and their bringing up, we can only wonder they have risen to so high a level, and think with shame of the little use we have made of our greater advantages and surroundings. This thought urges us on to try and do our work more prayerfully, humbly, and thankfully, for the privilege of being allowed to work, in however small a measure, for our Lord ; taking Him as our Pattern ; not looking for results, though accepting such, should they come to us, with deep thankfulness and greater determination on our part not to be depressed or cast down by the many disappointments.

One great thing we have always to keep before us in our work is to try to get into the lives of the people ; in that way our work sometimes seems overwhelming. We must be ready to hear their stories, try and understand their difficulties and burdens,—in fact, to try and put ourselves in their place,—if we are to give them true sympathy and advice, such as may help them ; trying to lift them up, to make them look beyond their daily burdens, which are indeed to many terribly heavy ; not being content with merely a pleasant friendly feeling with the people, but trying to go beyond—to dig deeper, as it were, to give them something that will make a *real* difference in their lives. And here we might sometimes feel disheartened and be ready to give up in despair if we did not remember that the fault may be in ourselves ; it is that we are wanting in love and sympathy, or in reality in our own lives.

I do not mean to say for an instant that there are not good earnest women round us, sometimes where you least expect it,—women who are mocked at, jeered at, almost persecuted for coming to church and Holy Communion, who do indeed suffer "for righteousness' sake." A poor woman, only a few Sundays ago, on coming out of church was attacked and knocked about by her husband because she had taken her baby to be baptized.

Then, for ourselves, we have each to remember we are members of a settlement, a community ; we cannot each act for ourselves and apart from each other. We must be loyal to each other, or the whole community must suffer, and the work cannot be good and effective. We must be always learning, keeping our minds open to be able to learn, if we are to avoid grooves ; always trying to put out fresh feelers, grasping more, trying to comprehend more, and, above all, bringing a brightness, a freshness into our work, whatever it may be, simply doing our daily work "heartily, as to the Lord," with a real love for and sympathy with the people among whom we are living and wishing to help. Love should be the keynote of our lives, with an ever-increasing forgetfulness of self, if our work, in any true sense of the word, is to be Christlike.

Before concluding, I should like to say I am sorry it has fallen into such inexperienced hands as mine to write an account of this settlement. I feel I have had too short knowledge of the work, but, having been asked, I could only do my best.

If the work of the settlement is good, if it is effective, it is all owing to the late head, Miss Catherine Newman, who entirely organized it from its commencement, and by her own life and example showed how those who undertake such work should order their own lives. May God give us grace to follow and carry on the work, so ably begun by her, to His honour and glory.

ST. MARGARET'S HOUSE
BETHNAL GREEN

(LADIES' BRANCH OF THE OXFORD HOUSE)

BY

MISS MARY TALBOT

ST. MARGARET'S HOUSE
BETHNAL GREEN.

ST. MARGARET'S HOUSE owes its origin to a desire felt by the present Head of the Oxford House that the work done by that house should be supplemented by that of a settlement of ladies. The plan was proposed in 1889; it was taken up by the Hon. T. A. Brassey, a member of the Oxford House Council, and by several ladies at Oxford. A committee was formed of those interested in the work of the Oxford House to carry it out, and it was then found that the Cheltenham Ladies' College was also intending to found a settlement in Bethnal Green. It was agreed that the two settlements should be combined, with the understanding that, as they grew larger, they should separate; and Mayfield House was opened for this purpose under the joint management of the two committees, and under the headship of Miss Newman, appointed by the Cheltenham committee. Miss Winnington Ingram was—until she was obliged, to the great regret of her Bethnal Green friends, to give up her work—the head of the Oxford workers. The first Oxford residents will always look back gratefully to the personal kindness and the help in their work which they met with from Miss Newman and the members of the Cheltenham Settlement, and it is hoped that the two settlements will always do much work in common ; but the connection was from the first intended to be temporary, and, in 1892, when there was a prospect of more workers than Mayfield House could accommodate, the Oxford committee decided to open an independent house. After some difficulty a convenient house for the purpose was found in Victoria Park Square, and it was opened by H.R.H. the Duchess of Teck in April, 1893, under the name of St. Margaret's House, taken because St. Margaret of Scotland seemed to the founders to be as striking an example as they could find of the religious and social service which women can render, and which it was the object of the settlement to promote. Miss Harington, who had been a member of the committee from the first, and had worked at Mayfield House, was appointed Head of the house, and every one who has worked under her can testify to the wisdom of the choice.

The objects of the settlement are in many respects the same as those of the many kindred houses the establishment of which has been so marked a feature of recent philanthropic effort. They all seek to remedy the evils which come from the isolation of workers—the sense of loneliness which tells so much on energy and hopefulness ; the want of co-opera-tion ; the necessity that each should buy his or her own experience, often at the expense of those whom they would help : and they do this by providing centres in which the experience and sympathy of many workers is available for the help of each, and from which joint work can be undertaken with the least possible difficulty of organization and co-operation. They make it possible for many to live in poor and crowded neighbourhoods who could not do so by themselves, and thereby to gain and give what all workers feel to be the inestimable advantages of daily-life intimacy with those for whom they work. And they can make use of the help of those who can only give short spaces of time to such work. In all these ways St. Margaret's House is justifying the hopes of those who founded it.

The house itself stands in the open, pleasant square which was the original Bethnal Green, and is thoroughly comfortable. Two large workshops at the back are good ready-made club-rooms, so that much of the work can be carried on on the spot. Life there is, by the testimony of all who have tried it, stimulating and cheerful, and gives scope for many different capacities and tastes. The house is already coming to be known as a place from which help can be asked and obtained in any undertaking for the benefit of its Bethnal Green neighbours; and many and real are the friendships that have already been formed between its residents and those whom they have come to help. Several ladies who cannot become permanent residents have given valuable help by short visits; others, living in London, have given one afternoon or evening a week to different parts of the work, and it is hoped that many more will follow their example.

If it is asked, What are the distinctive features

of this settlement? the papers which have described the objects and work of the Oxford House will give the answer. The movement, of which the two houses are the outcome, came from Oxford; its inspiring force was the desire to share with the people of East London the two things to which Oxford has owed her greatness—her religious faith; and her development of all the higher faculties—intellectual, physical, social —of her sons. Two things followed from this double object. In the first place, it was a Church movement: its promoters desired to co-operate, and, in fact, the Oxford House has co-operated, with the social and educational work of other religious bodies, and with many purely secular organizations; but many Oxford Churchmen felt that their Christianity and their Churchmanship were, after all, the best of the possessions which they wanted to share with the people of Bethnal Green, and that their settlement must, if its work was to be honest and complete, openly proclaim this fact. In the second place, they felt that a University Settlement ought not to confine its attention to any one side of the life of the people among whom it was placed, but to aim at raising their whole standard of living, and ought to lay especial stress on the duty of studying as thoroughly as possible the economic and social questions affecting it. These have been the aims of the Oxford House, and St. Margaret's House has been founded to promote them in all the ways that are especially open to women.

For self-invited visitors, its residents have certainly met with a very kind welcome. This is no doubt to a large extent due to the credentials with which they came : that to belong to the Oxford House meant friendly intentions and thoroughness in carrying them out was a well-recognized fact in Bethnal Green, some time before its ladies' branch existed. In the parochial work, too, which the residents undertook, the fact that they were personally unknown faded into insignificance beside their connection with churches which were known, by many who had never entered them, to represent a real wish to help and sympathize. And the people of Bethnal Green do seem to have an unusually large share of willingness to meet advances halfway. Partly, perhaps, because most of the outsiders who have come to live amongst them have done so with at least the wish to help them—partly from a certain neighbourly feeling, which seems to spring from the fact, noticed by Mr. Booth, that the native-born population of Bethnal Green is a larger proportion of the whole than in most other districts of London, and that many families have lived there for many generations—there is a readiness to believe in the good intentions of new friends, and to take as natural, and, therefore, trustworthy, the interest expressed in whatever affects the welfare of Bethnal Green. Reserve, suspicion, humbug, conscious and unconscious, are, of course, to be met with ; but real trust and affection—often taking the touching form of uncomplainingness for fear of burdening their friends—are much commoner characteristics of the ways of the people.

The work so far undertaken by the settlement consists mainly in a share in that of existing organizations, for there are few districts of London now which do not suffer rather from the inadequacy than the non-existence of attempts to meet the various needs of the people. But it has also started some undertakings of its own, chief among them being a Girls' Club, which now has three branches—one for children at school, which meets on one afternoon in the week ; one for girls under fifteen, who have left school ; and two for girls over fifteen. One of these is for girls of a rather lower social type than the members of the original Club—of the class which may best be known by low fringes, and hats either unusually magnificent, or conspicuous by their absence. Social grades are very clearly marked among factory girls, and it seems to be generally wisest to respect such barriers ; but this second Club, which has only existed a short time, seems to prove that the class from which its members come can enjoy and make use of Club life as well as any other. Different classes —those for musical drill and singing being the most popular—are held in the Club. Its management is vested in a joint committee of the residents and representatives of the girls, and it has lately been affiliated to the Union of Working Girls' Clubs. There has been a distinct growth among the girls of the *esprit de corps* which is so much harder to create among girls than among men ; and a very real friendliness exists between the girls and the residents. It is among these girls, and among their contemporaries with whom the visitors for the Young Servants' Association come in contact, that the most hopeful and interesting part of the personal work of the settlement lies. They are young enough for personal influence to mean a good deal to them, and hard-worked and sometimes careworn enough for the recreation and the sympathy which the residents try to give them to be about equally welcome to them. These things come first; the desire for any kind of learning is rarer, and so, of course, is the temper to which religion is an important reality. At the same time, the very fact that religious observances are not the fashion in Bethnal Green, makes any decided step, such as Baptism or Confirmation, a fairer test of serious purpose than it might be elsewhere, and, when it has been taken, it means real efforts and sacrifices to keep up to the standard that has been adopted. Such things as the abstention of a very regular and sociably inclined attendant at the club from the dancing evenings in Lent, or the wish expressed by another that one of the ladies would "liven ⸻" (her younger sister) "up, and get her to be baptized "—a wish which led to the desired result—are good signs of real convictions when there are no conventional standards to which they can be attributed.

It is sometimes thought that girls' clubs tend to weaken home ties; but, as far as the experience of the St. Margaret's Club goes, there is little foundation for the fear. The same girls seldom come to the Club more than twice a week, and it is a rare exception when sickness or need at home do not call out ungrudging help from them—help which is also very freely given to their girl friends.

With a view to keeping the broader aspects of the work and the need of study before them, the

residents and some of their friends have started a
weekly meeting for reading and discussion of social
subjects, for which, as a good many of the party are
members of the Christian Social Union, subjects
are generally chosen with reference to those brought
forward at the meetings of the London branch of
the union. As another means to the same end,
St. Margaret's House has lately joined with the
other women's settlements of London in a plan
of occasional meetings for discussion of subjects
affecting their common work, to be held in turn at
the different settlements.

Of the existing organizations in whose work the
residents co-operate, most are too well known to
need detailed description. First may be placed
parish work in its various forms—district visiting,
Sunday-school teaching, Bands of Hope and other
temperance work, mothers' meetings, district nursing.
There is practically no limit to what might be undertaken in this line in such a district as Bethnal Green,
except what is imposed by numbers and time. Then
there is work for the Charity Organization Society
and the Society for Befriending Young Servants;
visiting, in which all the residents take some share,
at the neighbouring hospitals, especially the London
Hospital, and at the workhouse. In connection with
this latter may be mentioned a Sunday afternoon
tea-party for twelve old women from the workhouse,
whose Sunday outing would otherwise only mean
an aimless wandering about the streets. In the
summer the work of the Children's Country Holidays
Fund absorbs the energies of as many workers as

can be spared to assist in it. In more than one of these undertakings residents in the two Oxford Houses work together.

It is always difficult and often misleading to speak of the results of work; in the case of a settlement with an independent history of not quite two years, it would be ridiculous to do so: but in the principles and the short experience of St. Margaret's House there does seem to be much to justify great hopes for its future. Every year's experience, every resident's effort to enter into the needs of those whom she is trying to help, will add to the fitness of the House to be regarded as a centre for the religious and social work of women in East London, and a practical witness among its people to the Christianity which would care for all human needs, and believes that they can only be met by patient personal service.

K

THE REPTON CLUB

BY

HUGH LEGGE

THE OXFORD HOUSE, BETHNAL GREEN

THE REPTON CLUB.

THERE is a class of boy in East London whose members stand at the street corners, usually in batches, and, when they move, progress in the shape of a gang which monopolizes much of the thoroughfare in which it happens to be ; they have been known to assault inoffending persons, and even to fall foul of the police. Sometimes these boys have work and sometimes they have none. Occasionally the close-cropped appearance of the head of some member of the gang suggests that the owner has been living at Her Gracious Majesty's expense, probably for fighting, or gambling in the street, or some other equally heinous offence. There is no mistaking the type of boy. It is quite different from the ordinary lower-class boy, and as a rule will not mix with any but its own kind. There are curious differences in the circumstances of the individual boys. One will be in good work, earning ten, twelve, or fifteen shillings a week, or even more. Another will, perhaps, never have done a decent day's work in his life, and would at first hardly do one if he could. Yet the two will be bosom friends, and stick up for each other in a row ; the one with money will give to the one without, stand him drinks, seats at penny-gaffs, put him up at his lodging or home, and do many other such things. One will be the son of most respectable parents ; another, without any place to call a home, or perhaps a home with the usual adjuncts of a drunken father and mother who make things hot for him, if he comes in while they are elevated, and are none too sociable in their lucid intervals, when he only acts the part of some one else who wants to eat.

One of my boys (who liked his people) gave me a lovely description of his father and mother. " My father, 'e *was* a man. 'E weighed sixteen stone, and thought nothin' o' sendin' you out at twelve at night for a dozen of oysters. 'E's dead now. And my mother—why I've never seed 'er drunk once! She's a queer woman. But my father, I've often seed 'im drunk."

They are curious creatures, these boys. If they like a fellow they will stick to him through anything. If they dislike any one, it is as well for him to avoid them. They are a class of lads from whom the army is largely recruited—tough, wiry fellows, with tons of pluck, and with first-rate fighting qualities if they are well fed and looked after a bit. I have seen one of my boys stand up, round after round, to a man far heavier than himself in a boxing contest, and get an awful hammering, but still stick at it, and never give in till he was hopelessly done up. And as likely as not this is done on the top of a little fried fish, or "a haporth o' pudden "—the horror of it!

I suppose many folk would consider the general

run of these lads as bad characters. This is an impression which is removed shortly after a first acquaintance. They *ought* to be so, considering their constant circumstances, but they certainly are not. If they have occasional lapses and forget the distinction between what is theirs and what is not, they could probably show that they kept one of the other commandments much better than a good many people do. One boy was recommended to me as one of a "regular thieving lot." Anyhow he and his brother—both under twenty—keep an out-of-work father and invalid mother, and save up some money to send their little brothers and sisters for a fortnight's holiday in the country under the auspices of the Children's Country Holidays Fund. I do not wish to maintain that they are all that is to be desired, morally or otherwise, but it is a fact that they have got many fine qualities highly developed, and just in so far as they possess great capacities for what is bad, so they have great capacities for what is good.

The difficulty is to get hold of them. They have a rooted objection to most forms of discipline, and a kind of pious horror for any man or thing that they call "religious." Their notions of what "religious" consists of are very quaint. One of my best boys—a well-known pugilist round here—who has never been beaten in England, and has just gone off to America to uphold the honour of the old country abroad, told me that he would have to take to religion out there, because he was going to stay at first with his brother's family, who "were religious and went to church on Sunday." He is a funny-looking little chap, with a great star over one eye, the souvenir of some hard-fought field, and, if he only knew it, is not half such a bad fellow as he thinks. His demeanour whenever we talked seriously together would have been a lesson to many worthy people I have seen.

Another boy had very exalted notions of what "religious" meant. One night (the day of the City and Suburban) I went up to the club, and found him there alone.

"Where are the rest?" I asked.

"Epsom, sir."

"Lucky chaps!" said I, "I wish I was at Epsom; but we don't have time for Epsom at the House."

"You wish you was at Epsom, Mr. Legge? Why, I thought you was religious!"

This was rather a nasty one for me, and I felt called upon to spend half an hour proving that horse-racing was not necessarily irreligious, and at the same time delivering a little homily on gambling, which made all the Derby and boat-race sweeps of school and 'Varsity days rise in judgment against me. The best of it was, that he did not think prize-fighting irreligious; but perhaps that was only because he did not want to hurt my feelings, as he had seen me at boxing-shows in the neighbourhood.

The club system is certainly the best way to get hold of these boys. You all meet as friends, and amuse yourselves together at innocuous pastimes like Tiddleywinks and Halma. It is quite a study to watch some rising young pug engaged at a game of Tiddley-winks. In forming a club, you first have to get a place to hold it in. This is not nearly so easy as it seems. It does not do to get a house in a respectable district—first, because the boys will not go to it ; next, because, if they did, the neighbours would soon object. Also, one cannot get a house in a rough region to which the boys are strange, as this would at once lead to a battle royal between opposing gangs, and the row would soon spread over respectable districts near by, which would say, " That's Oxford 'ouse," and complain to the Head.

After long delay I raised a house in a place which could by no stretch of imagination be called respectable. It is a narrow street, running parallel with a slum peopled with refugees from Shoreditch, who have been evicted by the County Council's Boundary Street Scheme. It rejoices in the name of ——'s Gardens ; and as the desirability of streets in this part of the world is in inverse proportion to the pleasing signification of their names (*e.g.* " Paradise Row," and " Land of Promise "), the sweet-smelling and many-coloured flowers and the smooth sun-lit lawns suggested by ——'s Gardens are about as like to the reality as a horse is to a hen. The houses on each side are three stories high, and the road is just broad enough for the dust-carts to go down it. Each pair of rooms at most supports a family, and the inhabitants are blessed with an abnormal amount of youthful progeny, whose life is spent in the gutters of the street, except when repeated solicitations from the school board have persuaded their parents to send them to school.

The house I found was like the other houses— three stories of two little rooms each, and a small yard behind. The vicarage supplied me with an excellent man, with an invalid wife and two small boys, as caretaker. They took up their abode on the ground floor. Of the first floor I made a bagatelle and games room, and of the top story I made a boxing-saloon and a bookless library.

The next thing was to get the boys. The Established Church supplied me with a nucleus of boys who were connected with the vicarage and lived in the district. The nucleus came as soon as the club was opened, and consisted of a very excellent and well-behaved set of boys, who were just like other boys. It was only a matter of time, though, before some of "the gang" should get wind of the club; and one night, after about a week's existence, two unmistakable individuals appeared, evidently to spy out the land. They departed shortly and returned with their friends, who certainly did not look a promising lot. They seemed, however, quite at their ease, took no notice of my existence, ignored the original members of the club, and retired upstairs to spend the evening, in what was evidently their wonted pastime, viz. boxing. I went up presently to watch them, and they certainly could box. I thought that I should be rather in a fix if I had to chuck any of them out. However, they seemed very good sorts of fellows, and were so astonished at being taken quite quietly if they made a row that they obeyed at once.

After about a week we got to know each other better. We had one or two little differences, in which it was necessary just to make it clear who was going to run the club, and then they settled down as if they

had been in a club all their lives. Their presence
soon had an effect on the original members of the
club, and most of the nucleus went in a body, re-
marking that the new-comers were too rough for
them. Oddly enough, it was mostly the smaller ones
who remained, and seemed quite happy with the
rougher boys, who were very good to them and
did not bully at all. I was rather glad when the
others had gone, as they were, on the whole, unin-
teresting boys, and not at all the sort my club was
meant for.

The new-comers, after they had settled down in
the club, went through various phases which were interesting to watch. For some time they did nothing
save box, but at last they went down to the bagatelle
room, and played bagatelle for a bit. They marked
this advance in civilization by prodding holes in the
ceiling with the bagatelle cues, which gave the ceiling
the appearance of a cloth target after a Gatling gun
had been shooting at it. I never caught any of them
in the act, so I said nothing about it, as they soon got
tired of the amusement when the ceiling was nearly
all hole ; but I regretted it in the hot weather, as
multitudes of the *pediculus vulgaris* (which thrives in
these parts) came through the holes and made the
club-rooms the scene of their nightly prowl. However, it is an ill wind that blows nobody any good,
and we beguiled many a weary hour hunting them
with bagatelle cues, thus obtaining a field for the
exercise of the boys' sporting tendencies, and eliciting
the interesting piece of information from one boy, that
" they live in the Queen's bedroom too " !

We soon acquired great prestige in the neighbourhood, and I got a good deal of reflected glory in
Do-as-you-like Street (as ——'s Gardens is known
locally) from the prowess of my boys, who com-
manded a respect in the place accorded to no one
else except " the coppers." As the boys got to like
the club, they brought their friends ; till we were
nearly sixty strong, and the crush in the little rooms
was sometimes dreadful, especially as one's eyes were
not the only things that made one conscious of the
presence of "boy." I had to stop the inflow then,
and regretted this much, as I could, if I had had
larger quarters, have raised easily two or three hundred boys, who would have formed about the finest
gang of fighting men in the district.

I had rather an appalling experience about this
time. One of the original boys, a very nice lad whom
I wished to keep at the club, had not deserted with
the others. I was sitting in the games-room, chatting
with some of the boys, one night, when I heard a
tremendous uproar in the boxing-room, and a loud
voice proclaiming some one's delinquencies in the
purest Bethnal Green. I rushed upstairs, expecting
to find a fearful fight going on, and was obstructed by
a huge black form shutting up the whole doorway of
the boxing-room, and apparently emitting the sounds
that had attracted me. The form backed out, dragging
some one with it ; and I then saw that it was a member
of the gentler sex, who had the above-mentioned boy
in a vice-like grasp, and, while belabouring him with
her disengaged hand, was delivering an eloquent discourse on my club, my boys, and (when she viewed

me) myself. I expostulated, and she swore ; and
I followed her downstairs threatening actions for
trespass and anything else that came into my head.
However, she got out with her prisoner, and I then
found that she was his mother, and did not approve
of his belonging to such a lot as me and mine. My
boys manifested a strong desire to go and take
vengeance on the coffee-shop which she kept, but
matters calmed down, and her son afterwards joined
our large boys' club, to which he was really much
more suited, and which he has since told me he
considers "all right." After the boys arrived at the
bagatelle stage, progress was rapid, and we soon got
to the stage when a committee was possible. I had
to go up to Oxford for ten days, and was rather
chary of leaving a stranger in charge. Moreover,
there was no stranger to leave in charge ; so I sent
for four boys, whom I considered fit and proper
persons, and told them I was going to leave them
in control of the club for ten days. The boy I chose
as chief of the four was one of "the boys" of a well-
known local sport, and was rising into pugilistic
fame ; while two of the others were like unto him.
One of these two was, when he first joined, the most
difficult boy to manage in the club, being the wag
of the gang, and so he was *a priori*, one of those
most fitted to be in command of the others. I gave
them a suitable discourse and went. When I returned
from Oxford, I was a little anxious. When I went
round to the club, my anxiety was soon dispelled.
I found the club had gone splendidly and in perfect
order, with an average attendance of about thirty,

and, on examining the bagatelle lists, I found that the smaller boys had had their full share of play. I sent for my four gentlemen, and thanked them. The lad who had been in charge described what had happened, and how there had been no rows at all, except with one boy who had made himself liable to be chucked out. As their way of chucking out is head first downstairs, I was rather glad the place had kept quiet. I then allowed the club to select four more committee-men, so that no one could say I only made the boys whom I liked into committee-men. Their choice was good, and made me more optimistic about the rising generation of the democracy.

About now a kind lady sent us some books. The committee thereupon considered she ought to be thanked, so I took a sheet of paper and a pen, and each one of them in turn gave me a sentence towards forming a letter. The result was one of the oddest epistles that ever was written, and they all signed at the bottom—those who could not write properly having their hands held by those who could. I think that this letter will be kept by the recipient.

Boys kept coming up and wanting to join the club, but as there were very few who left, there was not room for many more. Also I had to be very discriminating in choosing boys, and keeping the club down to the proper standard. If once a club like this gets into a sort of respectable groove, it is done for. The boys get into cliques, and seem to lose their delightful free-and-easy independence. The richer ones take to wearing collars, and commit all sorts of deeds of the same kind ; and then the poor ones begin to feel out of it, and to think their friends are getting too smart for them. There is no reason whatever, if only due precautions are taken, why such a thing should happen. The boys are much nicer in their natural sphere of comparative roughness, and are none the better for indulging in pomps and vanities which they cannot afford. Besides, the silk scarf and the amazing fringe they affect are rather picturesque. The great secret, however, of keeping the club in the right condition is to encourage the boxing. If the boys take to coming to the club in their Sunday best (if they have one), they will be more careful of taking off their jackets and having a set-to with the gloves. Now the ethics of boxing are these : (1) If a lad knows well how to use his fists, he, as. an almost universal rule, does not use his boots or a knife. (2) The discipline of the ring is almost the only discipline these lads get. That discipline is very strict, both in training, and during the progress of a contest. I have never been more struck by anything than the orderliness and good management of a well-known boxing centre near here which was controlled entirely by patrons of the noble art, and whose audience consisted of quite the roughest lot I have ever seen. (3) A man gets a high sense of fairness and honour from being accustomed to rules which disqualify him for a foul, forbid him to strike another fellow when down, and abhor such a thing as knuckle-dusters. (4) It is noticeable, and I have often heard it remarked down here, that the best men with their fists will often put up with a deal more provocation than ordinary persons, as if, being conscious of their power, they have also been taught how to control it. An old prize-fighter told me that the encouragement now being given in the army to boxing is having a distinct effect in making soldiers use their hands in a row, instead of lacing about with their brass-loaded belts. (5) The effect on the physique of the lads is great. If they did not box they would do nothing, and the result of doing nothing in Bethnal Green generally is oakum-picking. (6) Boxing is good for the morals. I do not mean that my boys are at all saintlike in *every* way, but still I am absolutely certain that they are a deal better than the ordinary street cadger and loafer, for it is to their advantage to keep fit, and more strength and stamina mean more money.

That is why boxing is good for my boys, and when we get a bigger place we shall have a fine boxing-saloon in it. At present, the little room where they spar is becoming rather dilapidated. There is a hole in the lath-and-plaster wall where one lad had his head knocked through (it did not hurt his head) ; and the chimney-piece came down the other day, and was shattered to fragments. However, we still manage to have jolly good shows, and visitors to the Oxford House generally have a look in at my boys. Some ladies, who were interested in the club, came the other day, and my boys got up their best show for them. The advent of a hansom cab in ——'s Gardens created vast excitement among the aborigines, and I thought at first that we should have to sally forth to a rescue, but it was all right, and our fair visitors expressed themselves highly pleased with the entertainment.

On one occasion one of my committee-men came up to me, and said there was a queer chap coming to join the club. I asked about him. "'E works in our place" (a glass-factory); "and one day we tied 'im up to a beam by the neck, and 'is face got black, and 'is eyes was comin' out when we cut 'im down, and it took an hour before 'e was 'imself again." I thought this was a curious way of showing a fellow that there was no ill feeling, and remarked accordingly. He thought not, and said that was nothing to what they had done a few days after. I inquired anxiously. "'E was lyin' asleep on a box, and we took a can o' paraffin and poured it round 'im and lit it, and lor, yer ought to 'a seen 'im git off that box!" I wondered what manner of man this new member was going to be. He appeared, and was evidently great friends with all the boys. I afterwards learnt that he was out of work and starving, and the only way he ever got money was through the boy who told me the above curdling tale. This boy gave up his work (stoking in the glass-works) one day a week, so that the out-of-work boy could take the job for the day and get the money. After that I concluded that what has been mentioned above was only a rather eccentric way of putting him at his ease when he made his broken visits to the workshop.

The last great event in the club's history was the seaside camp. Six boys came, and were put in 'a tent with nine from our other club. The first day of glorious freedom was a Sunday, and they broke every

L

rule in the camp statute-book. They did not make their beds, nor do up and clean their tent; they cut first church parade; had a fight with the rustics, and also with some boys from another mission in camp. The only right thing they did was to be in time for dinner. I went to them in my wrath. They were hugely pleased with themselves, and one said, "We met a lot o' them country blokes, and they got passin' remarks, so we gave 'em summat." I had seen them giving people "summat" in Bethnal Green, and was sorry for the "country blokes." I jawed them, ending by saying that these things must cease or they would go home next day. They then became very penitent, and all turned up in a lump at afternoon church parade. They marched to church with Prayer-books under their arms, and, to my intense relief, after chatting amiably through the service, fell fast asleep in the sermon. They did not miss anything. For the rest of the week they were models *in camp*, but concerning their doings abroad I "hæ me doots." One of them was very shy of bathing in the sea, because he thought the kippers would bite his toes. They were amazingly ill in a boat on the sea, and thought they were going to the bottom when out on a roughish day; but they had a rare good time, and I expect more than one of them had the first real good square meal of his life. One pathetically remarked that he "wouldn't get so much grub when he got back to Bethnal Green." I fear that he wouldn't, and the worst of it is that most of them wouldn't. How they live I cannot conceive, in many cases. Their charity to each other

is boundless, as far as their means go ; but even that
means a real hard time for the out-of-works. I wish
some one would make a point of supplying such lads
with work. They would make splendid fellows, and
if they got to like you would stick to you through
anything ; but I always shiver when I think of a life
spent on " fried fish and a haporth o' pudden."

THE OXFORD HOUSE

AND

THE ORGANIZATION OF CHARITY

BY

W. A. BAILWARD

THE OXFORD HOUSE, BETHNAL GREEN

THE OXFORD HOUSE

AND

THE ORGANIZATION OF CHARITY.

THE Oxford House has from the first taken an active part in the organization of charity in the East End, and it is as an old member of the Oxford House that the writer would sketch some of the work that has been done, and indicate some of the principles upon which the organization of charity is based.

He well remembers how he himself came down, many years ago, to the old House in St. Andrew's Street, anxious to take some part in its work, and how the then head told him off "to organize charity," the honorary secretaryship of the local committee being vacant at the time. He had not then a very distinct idea of what "to organize charity" meant; however, he presented himself obediently to the Bethnal Green committee, and offered them his services without the smallest regard to the fact that he had absolutely no qualifications for the post. He remembers a fleeting interview with the retiring honorary secretary, at which he asked what his duties would be; and he also remembers that the reply was "Chiefly to raise money." These were the instructions with which he commenced operations, and he inferred that the Charity Organization Society was a relief society, and that the best way to improve the conditions of the poor was to raise and give away as much relief as possible. He merely relates some of his earlier impressions, because he believes that they are those of many others when they first take up the work.

Since those days many Oxford House men have passed through some of the East End committees in the capacity of secretaries, treasurers, or visitors. Some have stayed for a year or more, others only for months or weeks. All have contributed in some measure to forward the work in the East End, and have themselves had the opportunity of gaining something more than a superficial view of the problem of the relief of distress. Both in Hackney and Bethnal Green, and in a less degree in Poplar and Mile End, they have worked at district committees, and undoubtedly the better footing upon which the society now stands in the neighbourhood is greatly due to their services. In Hackney, for instance, they organized a system of registration of relief which reduced the danger of overlapping to a minimum, and in doing so they brought the clergy and ministers of all denominations to recognize a common basis for their relief work. In Bethnal Green they have taken part in the relief work of various parishes, and have so formed a sort of bond of union between them. In one parish, at least, they have helped to organize a parochial relief committee working in co-operation with the local committee of the Charity Organization

Society.   In another, they have acted as collectors
under a system of provident visiting.   They have
repeatedly served as almoners of the Society for the
Relief of Distress.   As secretaries of the Children's
Country Holidays Fund, and as members of the
Sanitary Aid Committee, as Board-school managers
and Guardians of the poor, they have served to link
together the social work of East London.

They have, moreover, taken a prominent part in
the actual relief work of the Charity Organization
Society committees, by visiting cases of distress and
by carrying out the various means suggested for their
effectual assistance.   They have also helped in office
work and correspondence, in the raising of money
for cases, and in the keeping of accounts, and other
unambitious but necessary work.   It is, for instance,
in great part due to their exertions that the Bethnal
Green committee is almost entirely worked by
volunteers, and that its office expenses have been
reduced to a minimum.   But, above all, they have
made it possible to divest relief work of the taint of
officialism, and to infuse into it the spirit of personal charity from man to man.   Personal influence
and sympathy alone can prevent almsgiving from
becoming cold and mechanical ; in many cases,
especially those in which the cause of distress is
partly or wholly due to some fault of character,
almsgiving without personal influence is worse than
useless ; but many a case which would otherwise be
hopeless can be effectually helped when this is forthcoming.   The residents have also, by weekly visits
to the old pensioners of the various committees,

helped to bring a new interest into their lives. That their visits are highly appreciated is evident from the gossip of some of the old women who talk afterwards of "the fair young man" or of the "dark young man" who came and chatted with them so pleasantly. That they visit in no spirit of patronage or condescension is manifest from a remark recently made by an old lady who has in her day been a Bible reader, and, therefore, prides herself upon her knowledge of the clergy. "That young man," she said, "going to be a clergyman! *He'll* never do. He's much too retiring!"

As has been suggested already, most people begin with the belief, first, that the Charity Organization Society is only one of many relief societies, conducted, it is true, rather strictly, but still in its essence a relief society; and, secondly, that the relief of distress is mainly a question of money, and that with plenty of funds and plenty of good will, it is easy to improve the condition of the poor, indeed that it is impossible to injure either an individual or a class by the performance of such an elementary duty as that of "giving to the poor." They measure the need by the urgency of the request, and their success by the amount of material relief that they can provide or procure. If any doubts arise, they stifle them with the comfortable assurance that, though they may be doing a little harm, they are doing a great deal of good, and the reflection that "they prefer to err nine times in giving rather than once in refusing to give."

The great majority of people of the present day do not get beyond that stage. The growth of the belief that the question of almsgiving is one which requires study and thought is slow, and the application of principles is difficult in practice, and requires earnestness and conviction.

Those who have served even for a short time upon a committee of the Charity Organization Society, or have otherwise had the opportunity and the inclination to study the question at close quarters, soon realize that the question is one of extreme difficulty and complexity. They have, perhaps, seen those whom they thought they had " relieved " come back to them again and again with outstretched hands, their condition worse than before. They have, perhaps, watched the process of pauperization from the beginning, and have seen those who might have been independent and self-respecting citizens reduced by unwise almsgiving to a state of hopeless degradation, both moral and physical. They have, perhaps, seen instances of pauperism handed down from generation to generation, or they have watched it spreading through certain streets and districts where there is much almsgiving and relief, and they have come to the conclusion that money-giving is of itself powerless to stem the tide of misery and destitution. Sometimes, again, they find that, in giving money to one whom they have seen, they have been doing an injury to another whom they have not seen : that, for instance, by giving a mangle to a widow they have helped her to take away the trade of her neighbour, who has obtained her mangle by her own exertions ; and that the same principle applies to the giving of stock to small traders, which enables them to unfairly compete with those who are not subsidized by charity; or to obtaining work for one man " out of work " often at the expense of another ; and that wages in certain trades are kept permanently low because a large proportion of the workers are partly supported by charity or the rates. Or, again, they have been perplexed and discouraged because their efforts to relieve distress in any given district have made no headway—they seem to have been fighting the air; and the more they have given the louder has become the cry for help, until the destitution of the district has appeared to have no bottom.

These and similar difficulties force themselves on the attention of the thoughtful man who gives his mind to the question. At first, perhaps, he thinks that they are difficulties peculiar to the time in which he lives, and to the industrial conditions of the nineteenth century. Doubtless industrial conditions are responsible for much, and with them statesmen and politicians may have to deal ; but we must recognize also that a vast amount of human suffering is due to those defects in human nature which we generalize under the name of pauperism, and that pauperism is directly and immediately the result of indiscriminate relief. It is a question, not of the nineteenth century only, but of all time. It became acute in Rome under Hadrian ; if material relief could make a people prosperous, the Roman populace should have been so at that time, supported as they were by public alms from the tribute levied upon conquered nations. This is Gibbon's description of them: " For the convenience of the lazy plebeians the monthly

distributions of corn were turned into a daily allowance of bread. A great number of ovens were con-
structed and maintained at the public expense. At
the appointed hour each citizen who was furnished
with a ticket ascended the particular flight of steps
which had been assigned to his peculiar quarter or
division, and received, either as a gift or at a very low
price, a loaf of bread of the weight of three pounds
for the use of his family. . . . A plentiful supply of
cheap meal and a regular allowance of bacon was
distributed to the poorer citizens." And what was
the result? "From these stately palaces issued a
swarm of ragged and dirty plebeians without shoes
and without a mantle, who loitered away whole days
in the Forum to hear news and to hold disputes;
who dissipated in extravagant gaming the miserable
pittance of their wives and children, and spent the
hours of the night in obscure taverns."

It would be easy to draw an instructive parallel
between this and the scenes that occur in any urban
union where there is a lavish distribution of outdoor
relief, and it is well also to remember that the decay
of the industrial population was one of the causes
which led to the fall of Rome.

Again in the Middle Ages, the great abbeys supported vast hordes of poor, "valiant beggars" and
their unhappy wives and children, "dispensing," says
Fuller, "mistaken charity, promiscuously entertaining
some who did not need it and many who did not
deserve it; yea, these abbeys did but support the
poor whom they themselves had made!" The poor
themselves were the sufferers; their numbers increased

so that it became impossible to maintain them, and they roamed the country in bands, made desperate by starvation. Then came the dissolution of the abbeys and the necessity to protect society against the swarms of beggars; and enactments of extraordinary severity were passed, with penalties of whipping, mutilation, and death.

In the last half of the eighteenth century what was known as a "humane" policy of the poor-law was initiated. Restrictions upon public relief were removed one after another. Statesmen vied with one another in bringing forward measures intended to benefit the poor by making it more easy for them to obtain relief. Poor-law legislation was avowedly based upon the assumption that the poor could never be expected to maintain themselves, and must always be pensioners of the State. The workhouse test was expressly abolished by Gilbert's Act on the plea of humanity and economy, and every effort was made to remove the idea that there was any stigma involved in the fact of being dependent upon the rates. The result was that which might have been anticipated—the position of the pauper became better than that of the independent labourer, and the latter was fast disappearing from the land. In some parts of England almost the whole labouring population was on the rates, and the working classes were threatened with moral ruin, and the nation with bankruptcy. The poor-rate, which in 1785 had amounted to £1,912,000, was in 1817 £7,870,891, and it was still growing. Action of some kind was imperatively necessary, and the first act of the Reformed Parliament of 1832 was to appoint a Royal Commission to inquire into the whole question.

This Royal Commission marks a new era, of which it is impossible to exaggerate the importance. For the first time in history an inquiry was held under the auspices of a representative Government, which covered the whole field of relief. The commissioners were men of absolute integrity and impartiality; they were experts in local government; their inquiry was exhaustive and scientific—witnesses belonging to all classes of society, and hailing from all parts of the country, were examined. "The report," says a recent German writer, Dr. Aschrott, "is a masterly example of a thorough, comprehensive, and unbiassed inquiry," and it has ever since remained the text-book of those who have wished to study the problem of relief. It draws a vivid picture, supported by evidence from all parts of the country, of the state of things existing under the old poor-law, of the appalling demoralization of the labourers, of the increase of rates, which in one parish had actually overtaken the whole producing value of the land, and which in many others threatened to do so. It also points out the depression of wages caused by supplementation from the rates. The commissioners analyze and lay bare the motives and impulses which actuated both the administrators of parish relief and those who received it, and indicate the part that these must inevitably play under any ill-regulated system of public relief. They point out that to teach the bulk of the population to depend upon relief is to tamper with the mainspring of human activity. To

the vast majority the need of providing for themselves
and their families is the main incentive to industry
and labour. If that be once removed, the tendency
towards stagnation and decay sets in. They commence
with the declaration that the poor-rate was "applied
to purposes opposed to the letter, and still more to
the spirit, of the law, and destructive to the morals
of the most numerous class and the welfare of all."
All incentive to industry, self-reliance, and providence
was removed by the fact that the working classes
could claim as a right to be supported at their homes
out of the rates. No one need trouble himself to be
industrious and thrifty. The aim of the old poor-
law had been "to attempt to repeal *pro tanto* that
law of nature by which the effects of each man's
improvidence or misconduct are borne by himself or
his family"—a mistaken kindness, because "the
effect of that attempt had been to repeal *pro tanto*
the law by which each man and his family enjoy the
benefit of his prudence and virtue; in abolishing
punishment we also abolish reward. . . . Idleness,
improvidence, or extravagance occasion no loss, and
consequently diligence and economy can effect no
gain." And of the rate-paid labourer, "as his sub-
sistence does not depend upon his exertions, he loses
all that sweetens labour—its association with reward,
and gets through his work, such as it is, with the
reluctance of a slave." The sense of family obligation was fast vanishing; parents threw their children,
and children their parents on to the rates. In one
case a daughter actually claimed to be paid for
nursing a sick parent; in another, a woman who had

married a second time threatened to turn her children by her first husband out of doors unless a sufficient parish allowance was made. "The worst results," say the commissioners, "have still to be mentioned: in all classes of society the great sources of happiness and virtue are the domestic affections, and this is particularly the case with those who have so few resources as the labouring classes. Now, pauperism appears to be an engine for the purpose of disconnecting each member of a family from all the rest; of reducing all to a state of domesticated animals, fed, lodged, and provided for by the parish without mutual dependence or mutual interest."

The point which it is desired to emphasize from the above examples is, that indiscriminate almsgiving, whether public or private, is certain to make the condition of the poor worse rather than better, and that almsgiving is not necessarily charity. Defoe, nearly two hundred years ago, drew the distinction between the two in his celebrated petition to Parliament entitled "Giving Alms no Charity." At that time there were various proposals on foot for the assistance of the poor by public relief of all kinds, and especially by "parish stocks," or, as they would now be called, "municipal workshops." Defoe anticipates by two hundred years the criticisms that have been made lately with regard to certain similar proposals. He points out that the state, in giving work to one, only takes it away from another; and he holds up for imitation the example of Queen Elizabeth, who endeavoured to solve the difficulty by the encouragement of trade, and not by relief works. "' Pauper

M

ubique jacet,' said our famous Queen Elizabeth, when, in her progress through the kingdom, she saw the vast crowds of poor thronging to see her and bless her : and the thought put Her Majesty upon a continued study how to recover her people from their poverty, and make their labours more profitable to themselves in particular and the nation in general." And again, "The wise queen found out the way how every family might live upon its labour." And this was the reply to those who pointed out the vast crowds of beggars as evidence that there was no work for those who would do it : " Nay, the begging as now practised is a scandal on our charity, and perhaps the foundation of all our grievance ; . . . and people in England have such a notion of being pitiful and charitable, that they encourage vagrants by a mistaken zeal, and do more harm than good. . . . An alms ill directed may be a charity to the particular person, but becomes an injury to the public and no charity to the nation." He concludes that " 'tis a regulation of the poor, and not a setting them to work " that is wanted, in the truest interests both of the poor themselves and of the nation.

The Royal Commissioners came to very much the same conclusion as Defoe. After pointing to the melancholy paradox that all the legislation of the last fifty years, which had been intended to improve the condition of the poor, had had exactly the contrary effect, they proceed to demonstrate that it is the regulation of State relief that is required, rather than its extension. They do not recommend relief works, municipal workshops, or old-age pensions, but only that "outdoor relief to the ablebodied, inasmuch as it was the chief cause of the evil, should cease forthwith, and that the State should thenceforward confine itself to the relief of destitution, and not attempt to supplement inadequate earnings." It was a bold and drastic remedy, and the evil was deeply seated ; but the commissioners held a strong position as the nominees of a recently reformed Parliament, and, in the face of violent opposition, which culminated in several places in rioting, they carried their point. No one now ventures even to suggest that they were not justified by results. Almost by a stroke of the pen, they restored the bulk of the labouring population to independence. They, like Queen Elizabeth, had "found the way how every family might live upon its labour." The condition of the working classes began to improve from that moment and ablebodied pauperism rapidly disappeared. Their anticipations, in other respects, were fulfilled almost to the letter. With the limitations of outdoor relief the great benefit societies made an enormous step in advance. Wages increased, and, with them, savings-bank deposits, and labourers began to do what it was supposed they could never do, namely, to support themselves and their families in independence.

The report of the commissioners has been quoted from at length—first, because the effective organization of charitable relief depends almost entirely upon the poor-law being administered upon the lines laid down in 1834 ; and, secondly, because indiscriminate almsgiving is nearly as pernicious as indiscriminate out-relief, and for the same reason. From the middle of the century onwards the volume of alms-giving enormously increased with the increasing wealth of the country, and became an almost equally potent cause of pauperization. This, and the fact that there was, in the 'sixties, a partial reaction against a strict administration of the poor-law, led to a considerable recrudescence of pauperism, which attracted much attention. Professor Fawcett pointed out at the time, "that the growing pauperism was one of the most serious questions that statesmen would have to deal with ;" and, in 1869, Mr. Goschen, the President of the Poor Law Board, issued a circular letter, in which the respective functions of charity and the poor-law are, for the first time, defined. The memorandum declares that "it is of essential importance that an attempt should be made to bring the authorities administering the poor-laws, and those who administer charitable funds, to as clear an understanding as possible," to the end that, whilst the poor-law should be enabled to confine itself to the relief of destitution in the workhouse, "the most effective use should be made of the large sums habitually contributed by the public towards such cases as the poor-law can hardly reach." In this circular is summarized the whole creed of organizers of charity—namely, that if pauperism is to be restrained, the principles laid down in 1834 must be resorted to by boards of guardians, whilst charity concentrates itself upon helping thoroughly, effectively, and adequately those cases in which the application of the workhouse test would be unduly harsh. It was to bring this about that the Charity Organization Society was founded; and it is this at which it has been steadily aiming during the past twenty-five years. Once eliminate that portion of distress which is due to pauperism, and Christian charity will be set free to deal with the rest, and will be able to deal with it effectively.

But, in order to attain this end, it is necessary that workers amongst the poor should recognize, first, that there is a poor-law which is bound to provide all destitute persons with food and shelter, warmth and clothing, and that the treatment of the sick poor and of children has been enormously improved in the last twenty years; and, secondly, that dole-giving is a mere mockery of the better class of poor. This it is which the Charity Organization Society has, by precept and example, been endeavouring to bring home to those who wish to help the poor.

The progress made has been slow and gradual— much more so than was anticipated when the society was founded, and when it was hoped that all chari-table workers would be willing to act together upon a common basis towards a common end. No one is better aware than are charity organizers them-selves, that, unless they do good work, unless they can show that theirs is the better way, their task is a hopeless one, and they are fully aware of the great responsibility which rests upon them. But they believe that they have, of late years especially, greatly improved the quality of their work, and that mainly by the aid of the large number of cultivated men and women who have come down to the East End. And they believe, also, that this is gradually having its effect upon the general body of those who wish to "consider the poor." Co-operation upon cases is a fruitful source of organization. Many of those who were at one time most bitterly opposed to the Charity Organization Society, have, by this means, become its warmest friends. The clergy, especially, are beginning to realize that pauperism is one of the most formidable obstacles to their work of raising and Christianizing the lowest classes. The old prejudices are dying, though they are dying hard ; and whilst there are still plenty who criticize —as it is good and wholesome that there should be —still it is rare to meet any one who seriously denies that organizers of charity are sincere and earnest in their wish to improve the condition of the poor.

There are still some who think that the application of principle to almsgiving is incompatible with Christian doctrine. Charity organizers believe that this opinion is based upon a misconception of what organized charity is. If the regulation of almsgiving involved any limitation of Christian charity the objection would doubtless be insuperable ; but that is not so. Charity organizers would urge that the charity typified in the parable of the Good Samaritan is much more nearly realized in the helping of one poor friend, thoroughly, effectively, and lovingly, than in that careless almsgiving which squanders itself in doles : that organized charity means concentration and not limitation, and that its ideal is a much higher one, and one which requires much more love and self-sacrifice than mere almsgiving. St. Paul himself tells us, " Though I bestow all my goods to feed the poor, and have not charity, it profiteth me nothing."

There is one other point of view from which the question of relief may be considered, and it is one which is of especial significance at the present time. From what has been said above, it will be gathered that the whole question is largely one of character, and that charitable and State relief may be used as a lever, either to raise character or to depress it. It is an axiom of organized charity that "an application for relief can often be made the turning-point in the history of a man or of a family." At the same time, the great majority of the working-classes are happily independent of relief, and proud of their independence. Poor, they doubtless are, but possibly they are quite as happy as is "satiate wealth." Marcella, when she lived in Brown's Buildings, found that of two men living in the same neighbourhood, under the same conditions, "the home of one would be a heaven, the home of the other a hell ;" and the lesson she learnt was that "the key of the social question was to be found rather in character than in possessions."

We are just entering upon a new political era. The centre of gravity has shifted, and political power is in the hands of those who have not much time to read or think. Already we hear, on all sides, of all sorts of schemes for the abolition of poverty by State relief. The reform of the poor-law is in everybody's mouth, and "altruism" and "collectivism" are the commonplaces of every would-be social reformer. Relief works for the relief of the unemployed, pensions for the aged poor, free food for school children, are the chief demands that are made at present. It becomes, therefore, the more important that those who have had greater opportunities of study should make up their minds as to what line they will take upon these questions, and whether the coming democracy is to be based upon a system of State relief, or upon the industry and independence of the population. Already the increase of the proletariat (defined by Webster as "citizens of the lowest class, who serve the State, not by property, but by having children") is becoming a serious question in the great towns, and all history shows that it may be augmented to any extent by adoption of a policy of relief. It is not only the demoralization of one part of the population that has to be considered, but the fact that the pauper class is a millstone round the neck of those who wish to retain their independence. "To the rich," says Mr. Charles Booth, "they are a sentimental interest; to the poor they are a crushing load. The poverty of the poor is mainly the result of the competition of the very poor." When that competition is subsidized by almsgiving, it becomes ten times more acute.

This opens, of course, a much wider question than philanthropy can, of itself, find an answer to; still, it is one in which it has a great share and a grave responsibility. So far as that responsibility goes, the organizer of charity would say with Cobden, "Mine is that masculine species of charity, which would lead me to inculcate in the minds of the labouring classes the love of independence, the privilege of self-respect, the disdain of being patronized or petted, the desire to accumulate, and the ambition to rise."

Oxford House men can do much in the cause of charitable reform. 'They can, in the first place, study the question and convince themselves as to what is right and what is wrong. Without conviction, there can be really no good work. If they are satisfied that it is a cause which is worth working for, then they have exceptional opportunities, as men of education and influence, of spreading the light. They can, by helping to perfect the relief work of the Charity Organization Society, afford such object lessons in relief work as will convince others that theirs is the right way. They can, also, taking part, as they do, in all sorts of philanthropic work in the East End, endeavour to guide it in lines which they believe to be good and true. Again, as they are in constant touch with all sorts and conditions of men, they can explain away those misunderstandings which too often divide the forces of those who wish to improve the conditions of the poor.

The Oxford House has before it a fertile field of labour as the centre of social work in its neighbourhood. Outside itself, there are a great number of sincere and earnest men and women at work in the East End, all with one object in view, namely, to mitigate suffering and bring about better social conditions. But they have, for the most part, been working independently of one another, and often in ignorance of one another's existence. They have spared neither their time, nor their money, nor themselves, and of their earnestness and good will there can be no question.

But have the results been commensurate with the work done? Has poverty and suffering yielded, to any appreciable extent, to their efforts? If not, and those who remember Bethnal Green twenty years ago will tell you that it has not done so, and it is certain that the local pauperism has very nearly trebled itself during that period, then there must be some reason for the failure. Is it unreasonable to look for this in the fact that they have been working in the dark and with no system; that they have had no opportunity of learning from each other's failures, and of being guided by each other's experience? If the Oxford House can succeed in drawing together the scattered threads of East End philanthropy, if it can succeed in giving backbone to that which is at present invertebrate, its influence for good will be felt far beyond the limits of those social undertakings which it itself directly organizes.

SHELTERS

BY

THE REV. O. JAY

MAGDALEN COLLEGE MISSION
(HOLY TRINITY, SHOREDITCH)

SHELTERS.

WE all know the old incident of the loquacious traveller who once got on the box-seat of a north-country coach. "What," he asked of the driver, "is that castle yonder?" "I do not know." "What," he went on "is the name of that wood?" "I do not know." "What," he inquired a little later, "is the town we are passing?" "I do not know." At last he burst out, "Do you know anything?" "Yes," was the calm retort, "I know how to drive." It would be well if all would act on such a line, and admit that it is better to know one thing thoroughly and do it, than to make a pretence of universal and impossible knowledge.

In no sphere of action is accurate knowledge more essential and less common than in that branch of human undertaking which is termed philanthropy. An oculist must know something of the eye, a dentist must have some acquaintance with teeth, a cobbler even must know how to mend a shoe, but a philanthropist may work his fatal way upon all with whom he comes in contact, alleging only that he has a good heart: the rejoinder is obvious, "Why such a poor head?" It may be philanthropy in action to ruin a whole district by wholesale relief, but it is equally moral homicide in fact.

Now philanthropy run wild could evoke no easier method of pleasing itself and harming others than the idea of providing free lodgings for the idle and the dissolute. In order that some half-tipsy moucher may have the wherewithal to become at pleasure entirely inebriated would seem a poor plea for providing free shelters; philanthropy alters all that, and puts it in a different form : Let us, it asserts, provide free shelters; if they are abused the blame rests not with us who so blamelessly provide them, but with those who culpably misuse them. And this is precisely where the blame does not apply. As well tempt the poor tired donkeys of Sakkarah with loads of the fresh green stuff that is being brought up from the banks of the Nile, and then say it is their fault because they can no longer run swiftly. Once indulge beast or human being with what is out of place and harmful, and you may pretend to say it is they who are to blame for falling into such temptation, but 'in reality it is you yourself who deserve the scourge.

But, then, on the other hand, it must be remembered that, though all indiscriminate charity is bad—both for giver and receiver,—yet careful, well thought out, discriminating charity is the most blessed of all good things. May this charity be exercised by providing free shelter ?

Now, there can be no question that, in the London of to-day—London, the epitome of a province and the vast colossal excrescence of city-ship—the one burning, vital question is Rent. The house-sparrows and the sewer-rats have their free homes, and their more or less free lives ; but human beings, nominally highest in the scale of creation, are tied and bound by chains of circumstances which seem to force them into practical slavery. How common a thing it is to hear even fairly well-off small shopkeepers say, "The rent eats up all my profits"! How usual a thing for the district visitor to hear the sick man moan, "All that worries me is the rent"! To keep a roof over their heads, that is the most specially ambitious object of most of the working class. Even for those in work, this is always a struggle and a burden ; but for those who fall in the battle, who are overcome in the strife, why, for them, and they are many, it becomes a sheer, a total impossibility. "A terrible question is gnawing at my vitals," I overheard a languid fine lady say once, at the Hotel at Coire : "are we to go to St. Moritz with two horses or with four?" A more serious question oppresses most of the semi-submerged, as each Saturday draws near : "Can I pay for my room, or shall I be put into the street?"

Now to house the homeless, if it can be done in a legitimate manner, is not only a corporal act of mercy, but an ordinary daily occurrence under the poor-law, for which every ratepayer is therefore morally responsible. But besides this ordinary housing for the night of the pilgrims of the road, and besides also the workhouse accommodation provided for families who desire to live or winter in them, is there any duty incumbent on us of providing a night's shelter or refuge for genuine homeless men in London ?   I purposely omit women, because theirs, though a harder, is unquestionably a much more difficult case : they can be best dealt with only at a few chosen centres, by workers selected for their special skill.   Men, however, fall into a different category : tramps, of course, can be best seen after in a casual ward; but, apart from tramps and professional beggars, both of whom mostly prefer better accommodation than that of a free shelter, and usually manage to obtain it, there is a large class of more or less respectable, homeless men in the London of to-day.   It is a cheerful theory—that of the well-to-do—that in this best of all possible worlds there need be no homeless, outcast class.   Only, unfortunately, there is.

There are men in my free shelter now who have been respectable, who are still (if that means to be ashamed to cadge or steal) respectable, and who hereafter, in a world where all our conventionalities shall have been swept away, shall assuredly be accounted respectable for evermore before God's Face above.   For these, and such as these, a board to lie on and a roof to shelter are actual boons.   And here let me say I am not speaking of what I do not thoroughly know.   For over three years I slept, myself, in a little overhanging kind of balcony-room, just over our free shelter.   Here I could see all that went on, and hear every word that passed ; and now, though I no longer sleep in this little wretched cupboard of a place, I see each night all who sleep in the shelter, and interview every fresh applicant for admission.   In relating my personal experiences, I propose to describe the nature of the accommodation offered in a shelter; then to describe who should and who should not occupy it; and, finally, to offer a few remarks on work done, and possible developments of it.

Now, first as to the accommodation to be nightly offered: it must be just comfortable, but not too much so. In our own case, we have a church, unique of its kind, upstairs; beneath it, I built a large room, capable of holding a good many hundred people. This room is used for all purposes—mothers' meetings, Sunday school, concerts, men's club, and at night, for a free shelter. Why free? it may be asked. Well, fourpenny lodging-houses abound, and the Salvationists offer shelter for twopence; the class, therefore, who need seeing after, are those who can pay nothing. We have erected on two sides of our room a series of wooden bunks, approached by a ladder: to ascend this is always a good test of sobriety. For each bunk we allow one blanket or rug; originally I provided straw mattresses, but these became impossible, owing to the incursions of insect tribes. Each occupant of a bunk, if he stops over Saturday, has on that day to scrub it out; and each Monday, all the blankets are examined by the man in charge. We sometimes also douche the whole with disinfectant, or burn sulphur in the room. By these means, and by scrubbing the whole place thoroughly each week, we continue to keep comparatively clean; this is not achieved without continual carefulness and labour, but it is brought about by the aid of these necessary adjuncts. Besides the bunks, many men sleep on the floor or on a form.

N

For these, blankets are not provided. In summer
the windows, despite occasional grumbling, are kept
open ; in winter, a fire is kept alight during part of the
night. Throughout the whole year, one gas-jet is
lighted all night. The applicant for admission has to
come in before ten in the evening, and is called to rise
not later than eight in the morning. Opportunities
for washing are provided, and their use is obligatory.
Small as these restrictions are, men frequently resent
them : these are just the ones we desire to exclude.
"Will he brass up in the morning?" once asked a
disgusted applicant, alluding to myself. "No? Then
I will go somewhere else!" "He told me," said another
with severity, "to keep myself clean. I would rather
be in gaol!" But, upon the whole, these restrictions
work very well; without rule and order, a free
shelter would soon degenerate into a pandemonium
or descend to the wretched level of some already
existing places of this kind. What is wanted for its
inmates is firm, intelligent ruling, not varying from
day to day, but always the same. Another essential
for real success is, that some one connected with the
shelter should be always quietly, but sympathetically,
watching and studying each inmate. It is a poor
thing merely to herd outcasts together, and, perhaps,
nearly as unsatisfactory, to din hymns or preaching
into their ears and think that is all which is required.
Much more is wanted : for instance, we have a rough
labour test ; if a man professes to be anxious to work,
I always try him first, at some small job, and afterwards, if I can, try to get him more regular employment. Many of this class are very lazy; some, indeed,

almost physically and mentally incapable of continued
exertion. "Work," I have heard it said, "what is
that? something to eat?" But, on the other hand,
many are anxious to get any kind of work. I had
the whole of the interior of the church painted by
men in the Refuge, who were, of course, paid for their
work, but at a low rate, though we tried to allow
each man to work only one day at it. The work
was well done, and though the design was not theirs,
may even be described as artistically carried out by
the men. It is, of course, very difficult to get work
for those who desire it, but it can often be done.
We always make a strict point of one thing—we never
recommend any man without feeling confident that
he will be suitable for the job he is undertaking. In
some cases, indeed, a new comer will imagine that
because he professes to be "a good Catholic, Father,"
or, "truly on the Lord's side, dear sir," he will at
once be looked on as satisfactory; he soon finds his
mistake, and usually drops his protestations. As
regards religion, the only rule we have is, that those
who choose to stop a Sunday in the Refuge shall
attend service; I can truly say their behaviour and
attention might put some well-to-do people to shame.
Besides this, we have other services, one for men only
on Sunday afternoons, which most of them attend
entirely of their own free will and desire. Another
thing we aim at is to communicate with the friends
of those likely to be benefited, if possible; in some
cases, by this means, we have raised those who
otherwise would have sunk to the very residuum : but
though willing to communicate with their friends, I

only allow a certain number of letters to be delivered to them, because, otherwise, such a place might become a paradise for begging-letter writers.

And now as to the kind of man who ought to be allowed to use such a place. At starting, it might be clearly understood that I entirely refuse the tramp class, only accepting the highly respectable working-men who come up to London to try and get work. A few minutes' conversation enable me to judge as to this ; though sometimes, if I am in doubt, and prefer not to run the risk of a very dirty customer, I will give a stranger twopence to pay for his lodging elsewhere. At one time the Salvation Army shelters used to send me many who could no longer afford their twopence to them, and wanted, therefore, free accommodation. Most of these seemed to be unsuitable cases. It is hard to brand any as incorrigible, but once admit the vermin-covered, professional loafer, who never did work, and never will, who feeds on the scraps he gets mixed up together like pig's wash at the low-class cook-shops, and you will have no genuine London homeless working men apply to you at all. These are just the ones, who most people profess do not exist at all. In reality, they do, only we are all too busy to find them out—one section of us running backwards and forwards to charity organization committees, where we boast of spending four or five hours without making a single grant, or doing anything at all, because there is no such thing as genuine poverty at all, and, if there is, there ought not to be ; and the other section so delightfully intent upon getting up concerts and meetings and speeches on behalf of universal, unsectarian, undiscriminating, and all the rest of it, charities. Now, when we have a little time to notice the real needs of our fellow-creatures, we shall certainly discover that there are still with us many homeless men who deserve shelter. The majority of these have been soldiers. I had a man in the shelter for nearly three months, who possessed some of the best testimonials possible. He had been a sergeant, and was a teetotaller ; when he left the army he thought he should easily get work. Gradually his stock of clothes and his available funds dwindled away ; he was very anxious not to go into the workhouse, and fortunately came to us. I saw at once that he seemed a most capable man ; he had a very high record, having at one time received the unanimous thanks of the Grand Lodge of the Good Templars and other bodies, for the services he had rendered to temperance in the army. Despite all this, we had great difficulty in obtaining him work. First of all, he applied for a place in an asylum ; here he was told he would have to wait for a vacancy. Next he tried to get a situation as porter at the Holborn Union ; for this place he was chosen as one of three, out of nearly two thousand applicants, but was not the selected one. At last he took a place, at good pay and long hours, as a barman. This work he greatly dislikes, but will stick to it till something better comes his way. Such a case is but an example of many like it. Sometimes young men come to us whom we persuade to enlist or help to emigrate. Others, whose capacities are small, can (if they have no rent to pay) just manage to live by selling papers or articles in the streets. Many, as soon as they get work, we pass on to Trinity Chambers, a lodging-house built by a lady next door to us, where they can get really first-class accommodation for half a crown a week.

Occasionally we are disturbed: once by an eccentric, who woke up in the middle of the night, and got up from the floor to bawl out, in stentorian tones, that he would "run, jump, fight, or wrestle any man in the room or in the world;" and, at another time, by a visit from the police in the small hours, who desired to see whether a man, who was wanted for a murder in Whitechapel, and who had left his home, was in hiding with us. In the shelter itself all conversation after eleven is rigidly prohibited, as otherwise political, and even theological discussions, would go on till morning.

Only once has a real Romany stopped with us— a fine, clean young fellow of two or three and twenty, whose name was Tommy. He had quarrelled with his father on the road near Bath, and came by himself to London. Whilst with us he worked for a little Jew, "a most perfect gentleman," as he described him, who lived in Petticoat Lane; but he soon tired of this, and went back to his own better and freer life.

We have had a lawyer and a doctor on more than one occasion, and many who have obviously had histories. With many, drink has been the curse and cause of their ruin; some can stand, and even reform until temptation comes in their way. For instance a man who had been footman in many good families, and had good references, stopped in the shelter a short time since. He was quiet, sober, and well-conducted. Before long he got a situation as waiter in a small restaurant, and, would, I believe, be doing well now, but for an unfortunate windfall. His uncle died, and left him £100. With the first £3 that was given him of this he got drunk, and the last we heard of him was that he was in a low public-house in Spitalfields, drinking beer out of a can in bad company, and asserting that "wine and women" were henceforward the objects of his life. When his money is gone, perhaps he may be able to make another effort towards reform.

Another victim of the bottle was a man who rejoiced in the Christian name of "Clarence." He was strong, respectable, and willing ; but never could get over the fascination of drink. He stopped in one place over two years, and saved £30. He spent it in as many days. He left us, after a period of enforced sobriety, for a good job. I only hope he has kept it.

To turn back now from the individual to the general, I think we may take it for granted that a free shelter can do good, and can be saved from doing any harm ; and if this be admitted, as all who know must agree to admit, we may take it also as proved that care and trouble—and these are certainly requisite—may well be expended in providing such really useful help for God's lowest and least.

THRIFT
AND SOCIAL INTERCOURSE ˙

BY

MRS. MACE

CHELTENHAM LADIES' COLLEGE GUILD

THRIFT

AND

SOCIAL INTERCOURSE.

IT has been said that "Socialism is Individualism run mad." Whether this be so or not, it is, at any rate, clear that our modern social reformers have come to one conclusion, viz. that no one can deal satisfactorily with their fellow-creatures in the mass. Work must be individual.

If we, clinging safely to our rock, are filled with pity at the sight of fellow-creatures struggling among the breakers, it is not enough to wave vague arms, like sea-anemones, on the chance of clutching somebody or something ; we must hold out a firm, unfaltering hand to *the one* whom we have marked as within our reach, and ready for our aid. Having helped him to a firmer footing, not only are our hands ready for another effort, but we have a fellow-worker by our side.

Work for the masses, as such, cannot aim at much more than clearing away obstacles. Here is plenty to do for a great body of workers, and this age can point with pride to a vast number who are bending their shoulders to the task, in Trade-unions, Boards of Arbitration, Charity Organization Society committees, Friendly Societies, County Councils, Church Congresses, and Royal Commissions. It is a noble work that of filling up the valleys, and levelling the mountains, and making the rough places smooth, so that the people may come with singing unto Zion, the Zion of righteousness and peace. But even when the way has been prepared, the people have to be persuaded, one by one, to set their feet upon that upward path ; and the first steps are so difficult that individual encouragement and help are, as a rule, urgently needed. Most of our East End work aims at assisting our brothers and sisters to surmount these early difficulties. I have been asked to give some account of a few of such efforts ; one in the direction of promoting thrift, and the others of establishing friendly intercourse with working people.

Wise heads and large hearts in all ranks are trying to solve the labour problems of the day, and to find a way by which the workers who will work can be sure of earning a "living wage." But quite as important is it that the poor should be helped to understand the best ways of using and of saving money when it is earned.

English people are proverbially wasteful and improvident, and for many years all sorts of efforts have been made to induce the poor of this country, *as a body*, to provide for the future. To a certain extent the obstacles have been and are still being removed. The people are lectured and preached to on the subject, leaflets are thrust into their hands, savings-banks open wide their doors. But there is much to be done in the department of individual influence and persuasion.

So we go round to our poor neighbours, and ask them to begin to save in our "collecting bank." One and all say they can hardly buy food and clothing, much less save ; and when we suggest beginning with a penny, they laugh the notion to scorn. No one has such a disbelief in the worth of "a few ha'pence " as the poorest classes, of whose income the despised coins form a considerable proportion. However, to please the visitor, and with many a joke at the absurdity of the thing, one after another hands over a penny, which is duly entered in the collector's book and on the depositor's card.

Monday after Monday the punctual collector calls, meeting on the doorstep the "rent lady " and the "burial club gentleman." By degrees the tiny sum swells, and a sense of the possibility of having something to fall back upon in time of special need creeps into the harassed life. For those who put by a penny regularly soon find that they can spare twopence or threepence, and freely own that they have not missed it ; and the surprising feats that the despised pennies can accomplish in the way of mounting up are a never-ending source of satisfaction. " Why, it's like a gift," said one woman, when her first savings were paid out to her; "only it's better than a gift, *there's such a relish with it !* " Another, rather better off, put in sixpence the first week, but gradually increased her savings week by week, except during an illness, till they reached 2*s*. 6*d*. ; when the sums mounted up to £1 she was advised to open an account at the Post-Office Savings Bank. She now, after fifteen months, has £8 in the Post-Office, and nearly another on her card. "I know it would all have gone in chocolates and toys for the children if it had not been for your coming round," she says, with such a smiling face.

The testimony of provident collectors is almost unanimous that the poor show more gratitude towards those who go round in all weathers to collect their savings than towards those who take round gifts. If the collector be unwelcome, after fair trial, it is almost certain that he is wanting in method or in tact. These two qualifications are absolutely necessary; armed with them collectors need fear no difficulty. A rebuff is so rare that the fear of one need enter into no one's calculations. I have been offered, with the utmost delicacy and politeness, "something out of it for your trouble" when I was paying out a withdrawal, but never have I heard a rough word. One Oxford House resident was not quite so fortunate when pressing the advantages of our bank upon an old widower. "No, sir, I'll not join," he was told. "I don't wish to be rude, and what your object in calling for our savings can be I cannot understand; but I've lived a long time in this world, and I've never yet found that any one does anything for nothing."

We have only three rules in our bank :—

1. No single deposit must exceed £5.

2. No interest is given.

3. A week's notice must be given before withdrawal.

The Post-Office, to which all our savings go, insists upon the first rule, which, so far, has given us no anxiety. The collectors pay over their takings, once a month, to the treasurers, of whom there should always be two, for fear of accidents. Some banks give interest; but, on the whole, this is found to be a mistake. The cost of printing books and cards should be defrayed from the interest, and when the accumulation is big enough to yield anything worth sharing, some equitable method of dealing with it could easily be devised and agreed to by the depositors as a body.

Collecting banks should be regarded as stepping stones to the Post-Office, and provident collectors should be the mediums between it and the people who, from various causes, are so chary about taking their money there.

I do not think it can be doubted that the system of collecting banks has a great future before it. It is still young, but in some places its rapid growth has been surprising; e.g. in one London parish there has been an increase from £79, three years ago, to over £400 this year. In another older bank the deposits have reached the large sum of over £1700 a year. It has been calculated that at least £10,000 are placed annually in the Post Office by means of this one agency; and yet the number of parishes which have a collecting bank among their parochial machinery is still very small.

The system is capable of immense extension and development, but it must be wisely fostered and most carefully safeguarded. What seems to me a very valuable suggestion has recently been made by one who has long given the subject thoughtful consideration. It is that "a central office shall be established, to which all collecting banks shall be asked to affiliate themselves, and which shall be governed by a council composed of persons of well-known experience in connection with these banks." This central office would supply information, would furnish leaflets and necessary forms, collectors' books, and depositors' cards. It would be willing to audit accounts, to promote the formation of fresh collecting banks, and possibly would be able to find collectors for some of the very poor parishes. It would probably be a great gain to the individual banks if they were all to merge their accounts into one to be opened with the Post-Office by the central office. In America, what is known as the Penny Provident Fund is developing very rapidly on much the same lines as our collecting banks, but with an improved adaptation of our Post-Office stamp system, which seems very successful.

The most disappointing part of our own collecting bank is the frequency of withdrawals; yet, in the present unsatisfactory state of the labour market, one cannot wonder at it. Firms "break" or strikes occur, and numbers of men are thrown out of employment. The uncertainty of work is a far greater hardship than lowness of wages. Whether a man is earning £1 a week, or nothing, the rent must be paid and the children fed, and so the small savings are broken in upon. One generally manages, without being too intrusive, to find out what the money is to be drawn out for, and sometimes one can induce the depositor to hold on a little longer. Often the money is drawn out to pay the doctor's fees, those East End fees, so cruelly small from the doctor's point of view, but which loom so large through the mists of uncertainty which beset the worker's path. Very often the explanation is that Charlie or Rosie must have boots, and, unless there should happen to be a pair the right size at the second-hand sale next week, money will have to be found for a new pair. (In parenthesis, may I say that, if it were realized how much good is done by second-hand sales, without any of that loss of independence that gifts too often cause, to say nothing of jealousy, our eyes would be more often gladdened by the arrival of bundles of old clothes and oddments of every description.) We can all understand that to keep half a dozen children shod out of a man's weekly wage is a hard matter, especially when, as by the irony of fate, the man is himself engaged in the boot trade, —most disastrous of industries in this East End of ours—disastrous to masters it appears, as firm after firm collapses ; disastrous to men, as is proved by the fact that many of our small householders refuse to underlet to men in the boot trade, knowing the almost certainty that work will be slack and the rent not forthcoming.

On the other hand, the money is often withdrawn for "the holidays"—a term which may mean anything, from a week spent at Southend to a family picnic at Chingford on a bank-holiday ; or a "beanfeast" largely devoted to the support of publicans, but with no appearance, as far as I have been able to gather, of beans in any shape or form.

There is a revolt against monotony among our working people, against that changeless grind of labour to which their forefathers submitted; there is a discontent which is no doubt sometimes "divine," as so many express it, but which too often appears most unheroically peevish and futile; there is an insatiable thirst for pleasure, too often slaked at ignoble and polluted fountains, but capable of being guided, crying loudly to be guided to purer streams. Alas! that in this, as in so many other matters, the age has not been ready for her children's needs. Much more might be done in the way of providing purer pleasures; innocent entertainment for whole families, especially out of doors—organized parochial picnics, field clubs to awaken a taste for natural history, and that curious passion for collecting which is latent in every one's breast.

And this brings me to my second point, the best ways of "making friends" with working people; the young folk, independent from the age of fifteen or under; and the men, so seldom to be found at home, so often shy or suspicious of interference when found there. I know a clergyman who, being anxious to have a chat with one man, asked the boy who came to the door if his father were in. The boy went off to tell his father the vicar wished to come in and speak to him. Now, the man had no desire for the interview, and yet there was no chance to slip out at the back. But native wit was equal to the emergency: "Tell the gentleman I'm drunk," said he, in

perfectly audible tones.   Yet no one is more sociable
and friendly than an East London worker when once
you get to know him.   The initial difficulties are met
in different ways with varying success.   Some rely
upon men's clubs ; but the very success of these
sometimes defeats their own ends, the men swarming
round the billiard and whist tables in such vast
numbers that anything like personal friendship between them and the club promoters becomes well-
nigh impossible.   The same applies to girls' and
boys' clubs, useful and indeed necessary as they are,
as a preliminary step, if we are to get any hold upon
the bright young lives.   One of our devoted East
London deaconesses opens her little sitting-room,
evening after evening, to a few big lads, her " body-
guard," as they are called in the parish.   They
accompany her everywhere, when not at work ; consult her about every detail of their lives, from the
purchase of new clothes to the choice of a wife ; they
even give up beer and tobacco at her bidding, and
give her all their spare cash to keep ; one young
fellow, now twenty-four, has just married, but he had
put by £100 through the influence of this kind friend.

Many ladies hold what are known as " Fathers'
Meetings," or small clubs, where they spend one or
two evenings a week sociably enough, with a party
of working men, over music and talk and quiet games.
The men are, under these conditions, invariably found
to be pleasant and courteous, anxious to please and
ready to be pleased.   Surely it is womanly work to
try and bring some little refinement and innocent
enjoyment into these hard dull lives.

Others find more encouraging results from inviting their poorer neighbours to their own houses, and being "at home" to such as cannot entertain them in return. These evenings are most popular; they cost very little, either in money or in trouble. Coffee and cake; a smoking-room for those who cannot feel happy without a pipe in their mouth; music—the guests are delighted to supply this, but it is as well to supplement the very innocent and many-versed sentimental ditties which they will offer by something a little more cheerful and robust—an intelligent interest in the subjects which make up their world, the state of trade, the result of the last strike, the proceedings of the County Council; it is all very simple, very commonplace, but out of just such ordinary materials can chains be forged, delicate, intangible, yet stronger than steel, capable of linking together class and class, Church and people, earth and Heaven.

THE CLUBS OF THE CLUB
AND INSTITUTE UNION

BY

T. S. PEPPIN

TOYNBEE HALL, WHITECHAPEL

THE CLUBS OF THE CLUB
AND INSTITUTE UNION.

I MUST begin this essay by definitely stating its scope. What I have to say will apply only to those clubs which belong to the Club and Institute Union.

It is enough here to mention that there are in London more than 155 workmen's clubs affiliated to the union; clubs, that is to say, which have been sufficiently well managed and soundly conducted to satisfy the scrutineers from headquarters as to their claim to belong to a genuinely useful institution.

At least 219 provincial clubs are likewise affiliated. The total membership of the 155 Metropolitan clubs is 32,845 men, which gives us an average of almost 212 members per club. We will consider for a moment what this implies.

A member of one of these clubs renders himself liable to expulsion from his club if he is guilty of acts of misconduct. A member so expelled finds it difficult, if not impossible, to obtain election to any club affiliated to the union, and any club that acquires an evil reputation becomes liable to expulsion from the union itself.

The implication, then, is, that there are in London

32,845 workmen who are, as it were, under the eye of this organization, the employment of whose leisure is, to a certain extent, and by their own wish, subjected to an organized control. So much for theory, it will be necessary to compare theory with practice.

But before going on to the much-vexed "Drink Question," for it is on this point that adverse criticism must be met, it would be well to inquire for a moment into the causes which led to the creation of a Club and Institute Union.

Some thirty years ago considerable prominence was given to the problem of the workman's leisure. Good people realized that, when the workman had finished work, he liked company ; that his house was too small to receive company ; that the publichouse was admirably adapted for social intercourse—frequently it was the only suitable place ; that the workman was apt to get drunk or spend too much in the publichouse ; that something must be done.

Therefore they put their heads together, and said that places, institutes, or clubs should be provided where workmen might enjoy social intercourse, but where they should not and could not get drunk. Many were the temperance clubs that were started, many that failed. The plain fact was that they would not pay. They were not self-supporting, and many of the good people had got tired of subscribing, and meantime the poor workman had begun to find them a trifle dull.

The Club and Institute Union was started at this time, and was due to a like impulse. Workmen themselves thought the matter out, and received much assistance from great men. Lord Brougham and Lord Lyttleton both served as presidents, and other well-known men gave pecuniary and other support.

But the same difficulty was met with here. The clubs were teetotal clubs, and would not pay. Advertisement, subscriptions, and donations were not sufficient, and the movement gave signs of expiring. Lord Lyttleton was the first to see the necessity of meeting the difficulty, and of reorganizing the union on non-teetotal lines.

Then the movement grew and flourished, and the clubs became self-supporting.

Once more postponing the question of drink, let us, for a moment, ignore the sources of their prosperity, and take a glimpse at the clubs as they are.

Whatever may have been the objects of their founders, it is quite clear that workmen's clubs exist for the main object of fostering social intercourse amongst workmen. This is also true of such clubs as are termed Political Clubs. In all alike we find billiard - tables, bagatelle - boards, newspapers, periodicals, card-tables,[1] etc. Concerts, and dramatic entertainments are of frequent occurrence. The music at such functions is usually bad, and the histrionic efforts, as a rule, in laughable taste, but both are quite innocuous apart from their dulness. It is only just, however, to add that some clubs make noble attempts, not altogether unsuccessful, to raise the tone of these performances. The management of these entertainments is in the hands of the entertainment

---

[1] Playing for money is, however, strictly prohibited.

committee of the club, and, where lectures are occasionally substituted for entertainments, the same committee will be responsible for management. In a political club, however, where lectures and educational work generally are more in vogue, the political council will be responsible for the educational work, and its functions will not clash with those of the entertainment committee.

Any allusion to educational work in clubs which have social intercourse and relaxation as their main object, may be somewhat surprising. It is, nevertheless, an important side of club life, and one which cannot be ignored. The educational work carried on in the premises at Clerkenwell is well organized and extensive, but my object here is to call attention to such work as is done in the clubs themselves. Many clubs have evening classes, at which such subjects as French, music, shorthand, and ambulance are taught. The last is far the most popular study, and in some clubs a very high standard of efficiency has been reached. Many of the clubs, again, have libraries,[1] and such as are still without them make use of the lending library at the Club and Institute Union.

Space forbids me to enter upon a description of a club library; it is sufficient to say that they are, generally speaking, well patronized, and contain many useful works. But the assortment is strange. I once saw a copy of "Cicero's Letters" looking sadly behind the times in an East-end club.

In the matter of lectures the political club far

---

[1] Of 155 Metropolitan clubs, 107 have libraries of their own. The average number of books in each club library is 577.

outstrips the social. Many political clubs have a lecture on alternate Sunday mornings, and often on one weekday evening as well. A considerable number organize lectures for every Sunday morning, and sometimes set aside one weekday evening for a like purpose.

Of the 155 Metropolitan clubs which sent in returns this year, 78 have regular Sunday lectures ; of these, fifty-nine are political clubs, and nineteen social. As to the audiences forthcoming at these lectures, it is almost impossible to secure even a workable average, since all varieties of number occur between fifteen and two hundred. The latter number, again, will sometimes be exceeded, if a magic-lantern is used at an evening lecture. Much depends upon the state of the weather and the reputation and gifts of the lecturer.

To assume a critical attitude towards the educational work of such institutions as these is somewhat absurd. A workman's club is in no sense to be regarded as a class-room, and the fact that any educational work is carried on is itself a surprise and a gratification.

The term "Political Club" has, among clubs affiliated to the union, but one significance. Political clubs are Radical clubs. I said before, that in any club, whether political or social, the social element is always predominant. But as the educational work of these institutions cannot be ignored, neither should the political work be overlooked.

Political activity is chiefly displayed when any election is in progress. The hall platform, usually reserved for the musician, mummer, or lecturer, is at the service of the orator. Canvassing is systematically undertaken ; bill-sticking and other such duties are, in like manner, organized. Nor is the club behind-hand in matters of local politics. The political club is frequently the aider and abettor, if not the originator, of what is so common a feature in modern politics—the deputation.

So much, then, for the activities of these clubs. A glimpse is all that can here be given, before hastening on to consider what is perhaps the most important question of all.

It is not, of course, enough to plead that, without the sale of alcoholic drinks, these clubs would collapse. If they do more harm than good, it is well that they should collapse. If, on the other hand, it can be shown that what was first of all introduced as a necessity has *not* developed into an abuse, or even that the reports current respecting these so-called "Drinking Dens" are grossly exaggerated, something, at any rate, will have been done in the interests of common justice.

When, at the suggestion of Lord Lyttleton, clubs which supplied their members with alcoholic drinks were admitted into affiliation, the council of the union took elaborate precautions against the abuse of this new privilege. The ninth annual report, for the year 1870–71, has the following interesting passage, referring to this matter, under the heading "Public-House Clubs."

"Circumstances have recently occurred, in connection with this movement, which have attracted considerable attention and discussion. There appears to be a desire, on the part of persons who have lost, or who have been unable to obtain, public-house licences, to open premises under the designation of "Workmen's Clubs," where, with more or less of the usual club arrangements and restrictions, the sale of refreshments may be carried on for the benefit of the proprietor. In one such case the club was affiliated to this society[1]; but the council, on finding that the management was very unsatisfactory, and such as to bring the club-movement into disrepute, passed a resolution to the effect that the name of the club should be removed from their list of institutions, and the fact was communicated to the newspapers. The council have been assured by the Revenue authorities that there is no desire on their part to interfere with the sale of excisable articles in *bonâ fide* clubs, where those refreshments are sold for the benefit of members only, and under such regulations as shall prevent the abuse of that privilege, or the creation of a fictitious membership."

The tenth annual report contains the following explicit statement in connection with this matter :—

"Several circumstances having occurred last year which rendered it doubtful whether clubs supplying excisable liquors to the members might not thereby render themselves liable to prosecution for the infringement of the Excise laws, the subject was discussed at the Annual Conference of Delegates

---

[1] The increased stringency of scrutiny would make such a mistake impossible now. All clubs belonging to the union that sell intoxicants must be registered under the Friendly Societies Act.

of Workmen's Clubs on July 20, 1872. This resulted in the adoption of a resolution, and effect was given to the recommendation therein contained by a letter received shortly afterwards from the Chancellor of the Exchequer, in which it was stated that clubs can avoid liability by adopting such rules as the Board of Inland Revenue might consider necessary, and by forwarding a copy of the same to the Board, for their information. This suggestion has accordingly been followed by clubs which it affects, and much uncertainty and difficulty thereby avoided."

Further, all clubs affiliated to the union adopt the rule that no visitor—that is, one who is not an affiliated member of the Club and Institute Union—may pay for refreshments. If he is introduced into the club by a friend, any refreshment he may require must be paid for by his friend, and infringement of this rule renders the member liable to expulsion.

But in addition to these regulations for protecting the Revenue, most clubs have by-laws of their own. Most, for instance, will not allow a visitor inside the bar at all, and even a member from an affiliated club will be compelled to show his book, containing his associate card and monthly pass-card before he is admitted to the bar, though this precaution may be occasionally omitted if the person in question happens to be a well-known member of the Club and Institute Union. In any case, however, he may be called upon by any member to produce his book and show his monthly pass-card.

But to all this it may be objected that, so far,

no guarantee is offered against members of a club abusing their privileges by drinking too much themselves; that measures which protect the Revenue, do not in any degree prevent drunkenness in a club on the part of its own members. This, of course, is perfectly true; but, here again, precautions are not wanting. The clubs themselves have by-laws affecting the matter, and a member who becomes intoxicated, or in any way disgraces himself in the club, at once renders himself liable to suspension or expulsion. Again, if an individual club is lax in this respect, and permits drunkenness and misconduct within its walls, their evil report will, sooner or later, reach the ears of the authorities at the Club and Institute Union, and the club in question will be rendered liable to expulsion from the union. There is no club affiliated to the union that is not keenly alive to this, and the result is that the attitude of the clubs as a rule is one that backs the efforts of the council in their attempt to put down abuses of this nature.

Yet one hears many complaints. Not an uncommon one is based upon the fact that certain clubs affiliated to the union are "tied to brewers." That is to say, certain clubs are, in the first instance, started by the help of loans borrowed from brewers, and borrowed on the condition that the club in question purchases its liquors from the company that has supplied the loan. The main evils resulting from such an arrangement are that the club may be compelled to pay a high rate of interest, and has little means of protection in case of being supplied with liquors of an inferior quality. Nevertheless, the phrase "Tied to the brewers" seems to be an evil sounding one, and much capital may be made out of it by opponents who wish to damage the movement in the eyes of an uninitiated public. Certainly the system is an unsatisfactory one, and has been recognized as such by the council of the union ; but the position of our critics will not be strengthened when we inform them that, for some years past, a regulation has been in force, that no club so tied to a brewer will be admitted as a member of the union. It remains for them to make the most of the fact, that the rule has no retrospective force.

But the question still remains, To how great an extent is excessive drinking prevalent? This, of course, is a very difficult question to answer. There are, however, means at our disposal which may help us to a solution.

It would be, of course, folly to assert that drunkenness is unknown in these institutions. Occasionally instances of intemperance do occur, and such cases are usually dealt with by the committee of the club and the offender punished, either by suspension or expulsion. Such cases are, however, rare ; and the real danger does not lie in the fact of an occasional lapse of this sort, so much as in the facilities for constant "soaking" which club life seems to offer. A man, for instance, may sit at the bar for a couple of hours and drink much more than he ought, without positively becoming drunk or behaving in an unseemly manner, or creating a disturbance. In this case the authorities of the club can take no official cognisance of his proceedings. His behaviour may be all the while decorous even to austerity, but at the same time he is injuring his health and impoverishing his wife and children.

That this is an evil which actually exists I am the last to deny. At the same time I affirm that it is an evil which is greatly exaggerated. There are many clubs in the union where it is practically non-existent, and in this matter it is interesting to notice that the people who know least about these clubs are the people who have the blackest and most definite charges to bring against them.

An enterprising and well-meaning person has, perhaps, heard about the club-movement, and wishes to see one of these clubs. He prevails upon a friend, who is a member of one of them, to take him round. He is shown over the premises, and what does he see? Workmen everywhere, unshaven workmen, workmen with the marks of their toil yet upon them, workmen with mugs of beer at their elbows, workmen playing billiards, workmen playing cards (not for money, as that is against rules), workmen reading newspapers or chatting at the bar, workmen drinking at the bar. Also his nose is assailed with the odour of strong tobacco which is being burnt in the bowls of fifty or a hundred short clay pipes. The premises, too, are large, somewhat dusty, and not very luxuriously furnished ; not squalid exactly, but, to say the least, homely. He has not, however, discovered that the rent of the premises is probably £90 per annum,[1]

[1] The monthly subscription paid by members is usually sixpence or sixpence halfpenny ; in a few cases a shilling.

P

possibly even £150, which may perhaps account for a good deal. He goes home with a jumbled impression left upon his brain, of beer-jugs, billiard-balls, clay pipes, unshaven chins, and general cheerfulness. The next morning he is questioned about his great adventure. " Were there many rows ? " Well, no ; he cannot remember any rows. " Many people drunk ? " Can't say ; he did not come across any one drunk, but a good many seemed to be drinking. Yet a week afterwards, should the subject of workmen's clubs turn up in conversation, his ideas will become the more decided, and they are divorced from the truth. " Oh, workmen's clubs—I know all about them ; I was in one last week—mere drinking dens, I assure you." Then the subject is dismissed.

Through such channels does information too frequently run.

In such a discussion as this, one piece of solid information carries much weight, and such a piece of information I have, fortunately, at my disposal. The following figures have been obtained by inquiries which have been prosecuted throughout all metropolitan clubs belonging to the union, during the year 1894.

The average spent per year per member of those clubs which supply excisable articles is £3 9s. 2½d., which gives us an average per week of 1s. 4½d., or rather more than twopence per member per night. Of course it is easy to criticize these figures by calling attention to the fact that all members of a club do not attend on a given night.[1] The effect of this

---

[1] The great bulk of members, *often with their wives and friends*, are at their club on Saturdays and Sundays. This works out to almost the same as the steady attendance of each member.

criticism, however, is considerably neutralized by two things: firstly, that this average of twopence per member per night includes all drinks supplied by members to visitors who are not affiliated members of the union ; and, secondly, that in this same twopence is included the purchase of mineral waters, tobacco, and in many cases food, which is a very considerable proportion of the whole amount spent.

A somewhat moderate expenditure this for "drinking dens"! These figures supply us with a far more rational basis of criticism than occasional flying visits of enterprising and well-meaning persons. The question, as we know, is a difficult one to investigate ; but the most rational way to set to work is to start with a cool and unbiassed mind, and attach their proper value to facts which have a significance that it is impossible for a fair-minded person to ignore.

Before ending, I must draw attention to such connection as exists between these institutions and Toynbee Hall. This is the only settlement of which I have an intimate personal knowledge, and during my residence there I had special opportunities of estimating the value of the connection it maintained with the Club and Institute Union. During nearly three years' residence at Toynbee Hall (from September, 1891, to June, 1894) I made a "special subject" of these clubs, and, of course, my time was mainly given to those in East London. Some time before I came upon the scene a conference had been held at Toynbee Hall which was attended by representatives from these clubs, as well as by residents of Toynbee Hall and others. At this conference the subject of education in connection with these institutions was discussed. But this was by no means the beginning of the connection between the Club and Institute Union and Toynbee Hall. On June 25, 1887, the twenty-fifth annual report, together with the president's address, was read to the assembled delegates of the union at Toynbee Hall, and it was in this year that the residents of this settlement put their premises at the disposal of the union on the occasion of their annual *soirée*. The twenty-fifth annual report of the Club and Institute Union has the following notice of the event: "The form of our *soirée* was this year altered with extremely gratifying results. By the kindness of the warden and residents of Toynbee Hall we were given the free use of the hall, drawing-room, and library. . . . An excellent programme of music was also provided by the kindness of Mrs. Barnett and her friends, to whom we are much indebted for the very pleasant evening which our members enjoyed. . . . We desire here to offer our heartiest thanks to the Toynbee Hall friends for the energy and enthusiasm with which they assisted in making the party a success."

The annual *soirée* for the two following years was also held at Toynbee Hall.

My own experiences in these clubs were very much the same as those of the ordinary member. As a member of the Club and Institute Union I had the right of entry into the clubs affiliated to that institution. As a member of Toynbee Hall I, with others, did my best to strengthen the club lecture lists by obtaining the services of capable lecturers to address the workmen in their clubs. The most difficult thing of all, however, is to get the club-man to attend such conferences, lectures, or "sociables" as are held for his benefit at Toynbee Hall. Shyness and lack of enterprise would be effective obstacles to most, while many who would willingly attend are, to a considerable extent, prevented by the lateness of their hours at work. The workman's club usually begins to fill at about nine o'clock. Eight o'clock will have struck before they have had "a bit of a wash" and finished tea, and after tea workmen are inclined to take life easily. Evening lectures in clubs seldom get under way until half-past nine.

But in spite of such difficulties the inside of Toynbee Hall is familiar to many an East End club-man, and some of the merriest evenings I remember have been enlivened by their conversation and songs.

I am convinced, however, that the best way of getting to know about them is by constantly visiting them in their clubs simply as a club-member, and not as a representative of anybody or anything. At the bar or in the reading-room there is no such thing as shyness or reserve when once they have begun to regard you as a club-mate and a friend. Any subject that turns up for discussion here will be quietly and unreservedly dealt with. If it is your wish to expose historical, political, or religious errors, you have a better chance here than from a platform. Or if, on the other hand, your object is to learn and not to teach, a few hours casual chat will teach you more of the lives, thoughts, and feelings of these men and others like them than the study of many books.

Ever since its connection with the Club and Institute Union, Toynbee Hall has emphasized this side of its work—a work which, although it does not figure on the statistical pages of annual reports, is none the less a necessary element in all endeavour of this sort, and, at the same time, is most far-reaching in its results.

One word in conclusion. It should never be lost sight of that the Club and Institute Union is an organization that is essentially created *by the people for the people;* its strength as well as its weakness lies in this fact. It is owing to this that the club movement has survived so many difficulties and persevered often in spite of terrible odds. But it has not only existed through these thirty years, it has also progressed, and this again is due to its spontaneity, which is its strength.

I have pointed out the weak spots, and have carefully avoided exaggeration or under-statement. These weaknesses, where they exist, are incidental and not essential to the movement. As the working classes improve, so will their institutions improve, more especially those which are of their own making, and the spontaneous outcome of their own habits and turn of mind. Help and encouragement are needed here as elsewhere, and nowhere are they received with more kindly welcome and heartfelt thanks than in a workman's club. The converse is also true, for while candid though adverse criticism is taken to heart, unjust strictures are bitterly resented and long remembered.

THE FEDERATION

OF

WORKING MEN'S SOCIAL CLUBS

BY

GERARD FIENNES

THE OXFORD HOUSE

THE FEDERATION OF WORKING MEN'S SOCIAL CLUBS: WHAT IT IS, AND WHAT IT MAY BE.

IN a preceding paper, Mr. Ingram has dealt with the model working man's club as it was conceived by the originators of the Oxford House Movement, and developed by Mr. P. R. Buchanan in his "Tee-to-tums"—the happy democracy, free from every kind of bigotry, political or religious, which aims at being a kind of recreative Whiteley to the workman, catering for his reading, his healthy outdoor exercise, his billiards and cards, his argumentative faculties (through its debating society), his musical taste, his dramatic instinct, and his "days off" (by "garden parties," excursions to Oxford and Cambridge, or elsewhere).

But the scope of Mr. Ingram's paper is necessarily confined. The three or four clubs of which he writes are models and types of their kind, and a striking testimony to the effectiveness of the ten years' work of the settlement over which he presides; but their usefulness is confined to one corner of one district in the vast Sahara of industrial London. The socially regenerated through their influence could not amount to more than the "two legs and a part of an ear" of the prophet; and yet the energies of the residents of Oxford House are absorbed in attending to their needs.

But clergy and philanthropists from all parts of London have made the pilgrimage to Mape Street; they come, see, and are conquered; they return to their parishes, or their districts, and start a working men's institute on the lines of the University or Oxford House Club. I do not want to seem grasping in the credit I claim for the settlement of which I am a member of a comparatively recent date, but I cannot avoid the belief that it is due to Oxford House, in an immense degree, that a working men's club from which the modern-day Erinnyes, alcohol, politics, and gambling are excluded, has become almost a *sine quâ non* of every well-organized working-class parish.

But clergy, as a class, do not possess the lamp of Aladdin; and a successful working-man's club is not made by wishing. It needs constant attention, tact, and resource; it needs implicit confidence and friendliness between the organizer and his members; it needs the knack of mingling on terms of perfect equality with the men, while yet, by some *je ne sais quoi* in himself, he shall preserve their freely accorded social homage. He, in fact, must be the *kyning* of the new feudalism which is springing up in this present time, raised on the shields of his kin, for that in their hearts and consciences they acknowledge his superiority. Now, to acquire this position entails an amount of time spent in the club which few hard-worked London clergy are able to spare ; still less can they find time to organize the cricket club, the football, athletic, and rowing clubs, and all the other sub-societies which a prosperous club should possess.

For, be it remembered that, in democratic London, a *kyning* is all-essential. It is a strange feature to those who understand club life, how utterly inept the working man is for running the concern "on his own." It is not only that he is unable to see, for want of experience, all that a club may be of service and of pleasure to him, but also that the jealousy of the best, which is inherent in democracy, prevents his placing sufficient confidence in any of his own kind to promote him to the control and guidance of things. The Athenians were not, after all, so unique in their treatment of Aristides. Jules Ferry suffered like things at the hands of the French ; some of our *soi disant* " Labour Leaders " will yet experience them at the horny hands of the trade-unions. In a self-governed club this democratic jealousy leads, in strange fashion, to aristocracy. " We want one of you Oxford House gentlemen to work it for us "— that is the reply of almost every club to an inquiry as to what their requirements are.

I have opened my article with this general disquisition, because it does not appear, at first sight, what place a " federation of working men's social clubs " could take in a book of essays the aim of which is to describe the methods in vogue of dealing with the social problems of proletariate London. I am sanguine, however, of being able to show, in the course of my remarks, that, not only is the Federation a very real engine of social regeneration, but that, rightly understood, and properly worked, it may become, *par excellence, the* crucible in which the " two nations " may be fused into one.

To bring these two nations to understand each other's thoughts, intentions, aspirations, and desires, is the first essential step in the solution of the social problem.

To the Hon. and Rev. J. G. Adderley and Mr. Harold Boulton, belongs the credit of having conceived the idea of a union of those clubs in London which were run on the lines so successful in Bethnal Green. A constitution was promulgated on democratic lines. Each club elects one delegate for every hundred members, and these delegates, with the chairman, the secretaries (who are always residents at Oxford House), and a certain number of honorary members, form the council by which all the activities of the Federation are controlled. Council meetings are held four times a year, when all general questions are debated and settled, and new clubs applying to be federated are elected, while the routine functions are placed in the hands of the finance committee and games committee, elected from the council, and wielding powers delegated by it.

At the present time there are sixty-five federated clubs, ranging from Canning Town in the East to Acton in the West; from Hampstead in the North to Nunhead in the South. And yet the movement is but in its infancy; a little assiduous work will go near to doubling this number. Each club applying for election sends in a form, on which it declares that it has no political object, and that it does not permit the sale of intoxicating liquors or gambling on its premises. It is also asked to state whether there is any religious test of membership'; but the existence of such a test does not necessarily imply a disqualification. Again, it has to declare whether or no it will adopt Rule XIV. of the Federation, under which any member of a federated club is to be entitled to make use of any other federated club on production of his card of membership. This rule is optional, but is, most properly, adopted by the vast majority of the clubs.

When elected, the club pays a capitation fee of twopence per annum on each "financial" member, *i.e.* on each member whose subscription is paid up, or who, owing to special causes, is excused his subscription by the committee of his club. This paid, the new club is entitled to all the privileges of the Federation.

As regards management, the clubs are divided into Eastern, Western and Southern districts, each with its own committee and secretary. This principle of devolution has only just been carried into effect ; but it already bids fair to increase the usefulness of the Federation enormously. Oxford House remains the centre for the East End clubs, while Trinity Court, Camberwell, has accepted the duty for those on the "Surrey side ;" and Mr. J. W. E. Robbins of the Anchor Institute, Notting Hill, is organizing the Western district with much success. The solidarity of the Federation as a whole is maintained by a united council, while many practical difficulties are got over by this grouping according to districts. In this matter of working men's clubs, at any rate, the East is at present far in advance of the West.

The first point of usefulness in the Federation, then, is the opportunity which it affords for the interchange of ideas, and practical evolution of details of club management through its representative council. I shall have something more to say on this subject when I come to discuss future developments of the Federation.

But the chief spheres of usefulness up to the present have been—

(1) The fostering of a love for healthy exercise through competition in manly sports ;

(2) The promotion of personal intercourse between members of different clubs through the agency of the "winter games" competition, in which members of the various clubs journey to each other's habitation to try conclusions at billiards, bagatelle, chess, draughts, whist, cribbage, and dominoes, the individual winners of the various tournaments receiving prizes provided out of the entrance fees, and the club with the highest aggregate of wins a handsome challenge cup.

The entry for this competition has been very large this year, and the contests bid fair to be interesting. As regards more active pursuits, challenge cups are given for cricket, football, rowing, gymnastics, and harriers ; while individual prowess is rewarded at the athletic meeting, and in the swimming and boxing competitions.

In many of these, of course, only a small proportion of the clubs take part; the difficulties in the way
of making manly exercise general throughout London
are almost insuperable, and will continue so until
Government sees its way to following the example
of the County Council, and permitting cricket and
football to be played in the parks under its control.
The London Playing Field's Committee have done
yeoman's service in this direction, and, working in
harmony with this body, the Federation has managed
to provide grounds for a considerable number of its
East End clubs.

As is only right and proper, the cricket competition is most successful; cricket clubs being almost
universal in the clubs.

Here I must mention an unpleasant circumstance,
for it has a bearing on the claim of the Federation
to be considered a regenerator, even in its capacity
as a promoter of games.

The committee of the Marylebone Cricket Club
have, up to the present year, kindly permitted the final
to be played at Lords'. Unfortunately the privilege
was abused last year, and a disgraceful scene took
place owing to some supposed laches on the umpire's
part. The club this year felt compelled to refuse the
privilege in consequence.

Now herein lies at once the difficulty and the opportunity of the Federation. That scene was not unique.
Only a few months ago the winner of the sculling race
at the regatta rowed home amid a shower of brick-
bats, and a noisy and tumultuous scene ensued upon
the righteous disqualification of one of the crews.

"Pot-hunting" is the rock of offence, and the Federation is striving to inculcate into the members of its clubs the true sportsman spirit. We are far away from the days when the ivy or laurel crown was considered a sufficient reward — far enough removed, among the working men, from the spirit which impels sixteen youths of the dark and light blue to toil and moil at the oar for weeks for the glory of their 'Varsity, and the κτῆμα ἐς ἀεί of the said oar. But the goal will be reached. There is a movement in favour of making each competition an affair of the club and not of the individual; the reward of victory to be a challenge-trophy to the club, and a medal commemorative of the event to the individual. When this spirit has thoroughly permeated the members of our clubs, the Federation will have attained definitely one of its objects.

It is worth while to make a point of this, for association in sport gives the keen enthusiasm, the putting aside of self in the interests of the community, the self-restraint and good temper in adversity which all go to form character, and "character" it is which requires to be developed in the East-Ender.

I have said that one of our objects is to aid the poor, struggling parochial clubs to attain some of the advantages which accrue to institutions like the Oxford House, and University Clubs which are backed by the pecuniary and personal help of those interested in the social work of the settlement. The Federation has various branches for carrying this into effect. In the first place, it has an "appeal account," from which loans are made to struggling clubs to help them to furnish and to obtain the necessary appliances. This is a branch which may well be developed in the future. At present the sum at our disposal is quite inadequate to our needs; but even so the value of the aid given has been incalculable. And I must not omit to state that, up to the present, every loan made has been repaid.

To take a concrete instance : three years ago the Federation lent £40 to a club in Shadwell to enable it to obtain a billiard-table. At the present time every penny has been repaid, principal and interest, out of the proceeds of that billiard-table, and the club has been able to get another, and more than half pay for that as well. This is only one instance out of several ; indeed, so great is the demand that at the present time the fund is exhausted, so that we shall have to suspend operations in this direction until some of the instalments are paid back. If any generous person or persons should feel impelled by the perusal of this paper to aid our undertaking, I would suggest a donation to the appeal account as about the most useful help he could give. I ought to mention here that the applications are all brought before the council, and they have the sole right to vote the money.

Another undertaking which the Federation has in hand is the formation of a circulating library. It is proposed to form a central depôt at Oxford House, under the charge of a competent librarian, and to forward boxes of books every two or three months to every club which gives its adhesion to the scheme. In this way members of the various clubs would have a chance of reading the newer and more ephemeral books without putting their club to the expense of buying them. And it is thought, in connection with this, that, by getting presents of books, reductions from publishers, and applying to this purpose such money as the public might be ready to contribute, a way might be found to supply those clubs who need them with standard works, books of reference, etc., at a very reduced price. At any rate the scheme is worth trying.

Again, it has been thought within the province of our organization to aid our members to make the best of their holiday time. In this direction the average East-Ender is terribly unthrifty. He will squander his money in a long day-excursion on Bank Holiday, the fatigue of which leaves him more unfit than a day's work would have done ; and when he gets his week or fortnight, he will spend it hanging about the streets or in the billiard saloon of his favourite public-house. Not that he doesn't wish to go away, but that when the ordinary routine of his life is interrupted, he "dunno where 'e are." The Federation intends to point out to him where he *should* be. We have a list prepared of lodgings and places of accommodation at different seaside and country places, each of which we can warrant to our members as clean and comfortable. We have made special inclusive terms in each case with the lodging-house keeper, so that our friend when he goeth his warfare knoweth the exact cost. And, in making our arrangements, we have been particularly careful to cater, not only for the gay and careless bachelor, but also for Paterfamilias, his better half, and his hopeful brood. There is not one of our later developments which has been hailed with more fervour in the clubs than this.

Perhaps this would be a favourable opportunity to say something of the summer Saturday afternoon. Last summer we had parties on alternate Saturdays to visit places of interest in London, which were, perhaps, more than moderately successful. Sir Richard Temple, M.P., was good enough to conduct us over the Imperial Institute, giving us, *en route*, a very interesting talk about India. (Our party of two hundred may be said, in this instance, to have fairly "bought" the place.) The Dean of Westminster and Canon Scott Holland very kindly took parties over the Abbey and St. Paul's respectively, and all these were well attended, as were also the expeditions to the Tower, the Zoological Gardens, and Greenwich Hospital ; but for the British and Natural History Museums and the National Gallery there were "no bids." ·

Next year we hope to get friends who have country places within easy reach of London to ask our members down. It will not mean much—permission to roam over their grounds and disport themselves in such ways as they please ; a little tea and light refreshments : and the pleasure given and friendly feeling engendered will far more than repay the hosts.

We are open to offers in this regard.

And as to the educational side ?

Frankly, education is not our province. If we were to try it, it would be resented by our members. Not that there is no need for it ; the ignorance of the East-Ender as to the affairs of the world outside his own narrow sphere is appalling enough. But when a man comes to his club after the day's work he comes for recreation ; he is neither physically nor intellectually fit for mental effort, and one cannot but sympathize with him in his desire to "play."

Yet something is done ; only we do not administer education as one would a horse-ball, but rather conceal it as one does the powder in the jam. Direct educational effort is confined to the offering of two prizes, the one for the best essay, and the other for the best paper on an historical subject to be read up from books provided by the Home Reading Union. But these two competitions find few to enter for them.

The Federation, however, supplies lecturers to such clubs as apply for them, providing in this way a considerable amount of miscellaneous information, *plus* oxy-hydrogen.

But we look rather to the club debating societies to form vehicles of instruction in matters social and political. As regards opinions, we are charmingly happy-go-lucky. We are prepared to supply, quite indifferently, either Radicals or Conservatives to open debates, and to permit members to follow their own judgment absolutely. But we believe that, in the long run, if they are keen on their debating societies, they will learn to read up questions and

weigh argument, and thus be led to a right conclusion
—not that we are, among ourselves, by any means
agreed as to which conclusion is the right one !

To enable the Federation to give aid to the club
debating societies, a number of gentlemen have this
year kindly consented to go from time to time to the
different clubs to open debates.   There are some two
or three members of Parliament and public men
among them, but the great majority are young
barristers.   I cannot help thinking that a very much
larger number would give us their assistance if
they knew of our requirements in this respect, and
so I take this opportunity of appealing to those—
and I know by personal experience that there are
such—whose evening hours hang heavy on their
hands in the West End.   There is no need to be a
Demosthenes ; a clear head and some little knowledge of the subject are all the qualifications which
are needed.   One night a week—one a fortnight—
one a month, even, and an experience can be gained
which cannot fail to be as interesting as the aid will
be acceptable to us.   This by the way ; I shall have
occasion to return to this subject by-and-by.

So far I have spoken only of the general debating
arrangements for the individual clubs, but this year we
are working a scheme from which I hope great things
in the future.   Three subjects, outside the area of party
politics, have been chosen to be discussed in joint
conferences of all the federated clubs : first, the question of the immigration of pauper aliens ; secondly,
the Gothenburg system of regulating the liquor traffic ;
thirdly, employers' liability.   In the first place, these

subjects will be discussed in the debating societies of the individual clubs, the Federation undertaking to supply a speaker who will open the discussion in a non-partisan spirit. Then the conferences will be held, one probably at the end of January, one at the end of February, one at the end of March.[1] The meetings will be open to all members of the federated clubs who care to attend, and speakers of note—those, it is hoped, who are taking the lead in the various movements—will be got to address them, and, what is just as important, to listen to the views expressed by the members. Is there not here, it may be fairly asked, the germ of a most important development of the Federation's work? Through this machinery we may in time give to our organization an articulate voice which will be listened to in the highest councils of the nation. When any great social question is stirring the nation, we shall be able to make the voice of a large body of working men, not engineered in the interests of any party, audible to the ears of those responsible for the government of the country.

So much for the Federation as it is. I think I have shown that it is a conception not unworthy to be included among the different schemes and undertakings set on foot to benefit the toiling masses which the other contributors to this volume have described. I have shown it to be essential to the full fruition of those social clubs which are of such untold value to the work of social regeneration. But my tale is but

---

[1] The conference on the Gothenburg system is set for January 24, and the Bishop of Chester and Lord Thring have kindly consented to take part.

half told.   There are many branches yet of human life to which it may lend a powerful aid ; there are wants and aspirations yet which it must satisfy before it can become, as one of its members expressed a hope that it *would* become, "the guardian angel of the working man."

And first and foremost, "where a man's treasure is, there will his heart be also:" I want to see the federated clubs used for the purposes of thrift.   At present no definite or satisfactory scheme has been worked out, for we are, take us all round, but poor financiers. But I cannot help thinking that the mutual loan, sick benefit societies, and savings banks which are at present worked successfully by some of the individual clubs would gain in strength if they were amalgamated into a Federation affair.   The clubs might be enrolled as separate lodges of the existing great Friendly Societies ; and certainly, when any national scheme of Old Age Pensions becomes a matter of practical politics, the club societies might be recognized as useful mediums through which the workmen's contributions might be paid.

The fact that his life's provision is made through the medium of his club will very much increase the value of that institution in the working man's eyes.

Again, the Federation hopes to do good work in the future in matters concerning labour.   "Boards of Conciliation" was the subject chosen for the "social subject" conferences last year, and Messrs. S. B. Boulton, George Howell, M.P., and Musgrave gave invaluable assistance.   If we can interest employers of labour in our organization, and get them in large numbers to join us as associate members, there will be a Board already formed which could do much useful, if informal, work in the direction of establishing a friendly understanding between Capital and Labour. A conference of the Federation, convened by men who are outside the sphere of industrial dispute, to which the leaders of both parties were invited, might do much in the direction of mollification and counsel, even though it would be necessarily without any power to arrive at a definite decision.

Closely connected with this is the proposal to establish a "Labour Bureau." The attempt was made some two or three years ago, but ended in failure, chiefly owing to the inexperience of those who had its direction, and to their lack of "touch" with employers of labour.

Here, again, we need to augment the number of our associate members very largely before we can do anything effective. And we must needs have too a considerable capital sum at our disposal to defray the expenses of office and clerical staff until the thing gets into thorough working order. It *may* be done, and it *will* be done. I can conceive of no organization better qualified by the very conditions of its being to take it up. But, *festina lente !* we must walk before we can run, and enthusiasm will not make up for lack of business training and knowledge of the world.

Another branch of public utility in which the Federation is well qualified to assist is in the administration of the laws on the housing of the working-classes, on the lines of the Mansion House Committee. The clubs round Oxford House already take a useful share in this work; we might through our organization extend the system till we have working-men's committees in every quarter of London. The municipal spirit is spreading; there is a common desire to see London a brighter, purer, more wholesome city. In such organizations as ours may be found the means of checking the deplorable spirit of political partisanship which threatens to wreck the development of our municipal life by subordinating the true interests of the community to the manœuvrings of party caucuses. When the Federation grows to manhood it will have its own utilitarian, non-partisan programme of municipal administration.

So much for what we are, and what we may become. I turn now to the question, What do we want? How can those living out of touch with the seething life of industrial London, too busy to give their time to our work, assist us? In the first place, by becoming associate members. This only entails the subscribing of five shillings a year. I cannot help thinking that among all the business and professional men of London there will be very many who will be ready to link themselves with our organization in this way. The payment of this sum gives the associates the right to attend the annual general meeting of the Federation, and to elect twenty of their number on to the council.

This is the minimum of interest for an associate to take; but he may do more, an he will. He may attach himself to a particular club in his district: go and help in its administration; run its debating society, its musical society, its lectures, its cricket and football clubs, and its ambulance corps. Whatever a man's idiosyncrasy or his hobby may be, we can find an outlet for it in our organization. Those who feel they cannot tie themselves down so closely—who, instead of giving an evening a week, can only give one occasionally—may enroll themselves on our list of those willing to open debates on set subjects ; or, if they have musical or dramatic talent, may signify their willingness to take part in concerts or theatrical "shows." I can assure all these that they will be richly repaid. I can say, emphatically, that an evening spent in a workman's club is far more enjoyable than one spent at a "crush" in a West End drawing-room. No one who has not met the London workman in his own special little domain knows what a real good fellow he is—can gauge the genial hearty welcome which will be accorded, the broad-minded interest he can show in points of view which are not his own, on all subjects.

There is no fear of the Bachelor Club young man feeling a fish-out-of-water at "Univ" or the Ratcliff Tee-to-tum. If he will lay aside the erroneous idea that it is a "condescension" for him to come, he will be met as man by man, as friend by friend. He will be gauged by his capacity for good-fellowship, and his power to contribute something to the life of the club.

To others—men skilled in business, men with their fingers on the pulse of public affairs, to Cabinet Ministers and Labour leaders alike—I would say, "Give us of your help and advice ; show us what we can do, and how it may be done." We will provide the machinery, and hearty, willing workers, but we want experienced heads to guide us, friendly suggestion, a helping hand in starting.

The prospect before us is almost limitless : who knows what may spring from the knitting and welding of all classes together in social intercourse, in pastimes, in discussion of great questions ? In working-men's clubs, free from the taint of the pothouse, with ramifications extending into all the manifold sides of human life, helping in the home, in the workshop, in the playing-field, Englishmen may be made one in humdrum days of peace, as they would be one when face to face with a foreign invader.

A SELECTION

FROM THE

Recent Publications

OF

MESSRS. RIVINGTON

1901

34 *KING STREET, COVENT GARDEN*
LONDON

34 KING STREET, COVENT GARDEN,
LONDON, W.C.,   *October*, 1901.

In November. *Demy 8vo.* 16s.

The Story of the Khedivate

By EDWARD DICEY, C.B.

CONTENTS.—The Founder of the Khedival Dynasty—The Reigns of Abbas and Said—The Suez Canal—Accession of Ismail Pasha—The Purse of Fortunatus—Ismail in his Grandeur—The Road to Ruin—The Credit Side of the Account—The Beginning of a New Era—The Cave Mission—First Stage of Intervention—The Second Stage of Intervention —The Anglo-French Ministry—The *Coup d'État*—The Deposition of Ismail—Egypt under Sigurddin—The Dual Control—The Arabi Mutiny —The Nationality Movement—The Chamber of Notables—The Military Dictatorship—The Massacres of Alexandria—The Bombardment—British Intervention—Tel-el-Kebir—After the Mutiny—The Rising of the Mahdi —Lord Dufferin's Report—The Evacuation of the Soudan—Gordon's Return—The Nubar Pasha Ministry—The Fall of Khartoum—The North-brook Mission—The Anglo-Turkish Convention—The Invasion of Egypt —Under British Supervision—The Reign of Tewfik—The Accession of Abbas Pasha—The Advance on Dongola—On the Road to Khartoum— The Condominium—A Retrospect.

Just Published. *Demy 8vo.* *With Map and numerous Illustrations.*
10s. *net.*

Chinese Turkestan

With Caravan and Rifle.

By PERCY W. CHURCH, F.R.G.S., F.Z.S.

CONTENTS.—Outfit, etc.—Srinagar to Leh—Leh to Yarkand—Yarkand to Maralbashi — Aksu to Shatta, in Tekkes — Sport in the Tekkes : Wapiti—Sport in the Tekkes : Ibex—Wapiti and Ibex—Roe Deer— On to Kuldja — Kuldja to Urumtsi — Urumtsi to Kucha — Kucha to Khotan—Khotan to Shahdula and Leh—Field Notes on Game : Game of the Tekkes.

Demy 8vo. 1s.

A Letter and Two other Papers

On the Water of the Great Rivers of India

as essential to the prosperity of the Nation
and the only possible means of preventing Famine.

After Seventy-three years of Study of the Subject

By MAJOR-GENERAL F. C. COTTON, C.S.I.
Late R.E.

London : 34 King Street, Covent Garden.

Just Published. Crown 8vo. 6s. net.

The Soul in the Unseen World

An Inquiry into the Doctrine of the Intermediate State.

By R. E. HUTTON.
Chaplain of St. Margaret's, East Grinstead.
Author of 'The Crown of Christ,' etc.

CONTENTS.—A Teacher come from God—Body, Soul, and Spirit—Is the Soul Immortal?—The Breaking of Dreams—The Witness of the Old Testament—The Witness of Ancient Greece and Rome—The Witness of Jewish Tradition—The Witness of the New Testament: Hades—The Witness of the New Testament: Paradise—The Teaching of the Primitive Church—Prayer for the Departed in the Primitive Church—Patristic Teaching on Future Purification—Teaching of the Mediæval and Greek Church—Purgatory: Roman Dogma—The Romish Doctrine concerning Purgatory—Anglican Teaching—Jesus, and the Resurrection—The Doctrine of the Holy Eastern Church—Index.

Just Published. Crown 8vo. 5s. net.

Studies in Holy Scripture

A Volume of Sermons.

By the REV. ALFRED G. MORTIMER, D.D.,
Rector of St. Mark's, Philadelphia.

CONTENTS.—Abraham—Isaac—Jacob—Joseph—Balaam—Uzzah—The Parable of the Sower—The Sons of God—The Training of S. Peter—Allegory of the Good Shepherd—Seed among Thorns—Character and Circumstances—The Soul's Question—The Body and the Eagles—The Victory of Easter—Our Light Affliction—The Powers of Evil—Humility—The Eucharistic Sacrifice.

In November. Small fcap. 8vo. 2s. net.

Thoughts on the Penitential Psalms

A Sequel to 'The Hallowing of Sorrow.'

By ETHEL ROMANES.

With a Preface by the Rev. H. SCOTT HOLLAND,
Canon of St. Paul's.

London: 34 King Street, Covent Garden.

Just Published. Crown 8vo. 6s. net.

Roman Law and History in the New Testament

By the Rev. SEPTIMUS BUSS, LL.B.,
Rector of St. Anne and St. Agnes, London, E.C.

THE object of this work is to present in a concise form the main facts of Roman Law and History as found in the New Testament. Special attention has been directed to the trial of our Lord, and of St. Paul.

CONTENTS.—Herod and the Nativity—Cyrenis and the Taxing—Augustus and the Provinces—Antipas and the Herodian Family—Tiberius and Tribute—Pilate and the Trial of our Lord—Claudius and the Jews—Sergius Paulus and Superstition—Bernice and Marriage—Gallio and Provincial Governors—Asiarchs and Provincial Officials—Aretas and Principalities—Claudius Lysias and the Army—Citizenship—Felix and Criminal Procedure—Festus and Appeal—Julius and Rome—Nero and Trial on Appeal—Titus and Jerusalem—Domitian and Patmos.

Crown 8vo. 4s. 6d. net.

Prospice

Sermons Preached in Clifton College Chapel.

By the Rev. M. G. GLAZEBROOK, M.A.,
Head Master of Clifton College and Hon Canon of Bristol Cathedral.

Demy 8vo. 1s.

Church Work and Church Reform

A Charge delivered to the Clergy and Churchwardens of the Diocese of Hereford at his second triennial visitation, May and June 1901

By JOHN PERCIVAL, D.D.,
Bishop of Hereford.

Crown 8vo. Sewed, 2d.

Christian Truths

Dedicated to those who are assisting in teaching and to all Learners.

By a TEACHER.
With a Preface by Canon KNOX LITTLE.

London : 34 King Street, Covent Garden.

Crown 8vo.   4s. 6d. net.

The Books of the New Testament

By the REV. LEIGHTON PULLAN, M.A.,

Fellow of St. John's College, and Lecturer in Theology at St. John's,
Oriel, and Queen's Colleges, Oxford.

'Mr. Pullan has given us a work which will add a fresh charm and interest to the study of Holy Scripture, and which supplies an adequate and trustworthy reply to the destructive criticism that has tended to unsettle and distress so many earnest minds.'—**Church Quarterly Review.**

'We have found it a pleasant occupation to read the chapters through, and can bear testimony to the ability and fairness with which they are written.   Mr. Pullan's readers will find that they are under the guidance of an accurate scholar, who is more anxious to lay before them the actual facts, so far as they can be ascertained, than to air theories.   His discussions on the sources of the Synoptic Gospels, and on the Second Epistle of St. Peter, may be mentioned as instances of this.   It is difficult to draw the line, but Mr. Pullan has done so with great care and judgment, and his book effectually supplies a long-felt need.   The translation of the Muratorian Fragment, contained in an appendix, will be most useful.   There is besides a well-arranged list, with dates, of the early witnesses to New Testament writings.'—**Church Times.**

'The work abounds in unmistakable proofs of sure scholarship and ripe judgment.   It represents the latest opinion of the conservative critics, who now hold the field of Biblical criticism, and it aims at setting forth this opinion in a plain, straightforward manner, so that any ordinary person of average intelligence can appreciate the position and the arguments.'—**Church Review.**

'It is, in fact, practically a popular handbook of the Biblical criticism of the New Testament, and is an additional proof of the remarkably good and vigorous work which the Church of England is at present doing in this sphere.'—**Glasgow Herald.**

'The style is good, the language picturesque.   In the work that lies before us of showing that the foundations of the Faith are laid upon the rock of historical fact, this welcome book should take a responsible place.'—**Expository Times.**

Crown 8vo.   1s. 6d.

Greek Manuals of Church Doctrine

By the REV. H. T. F. DUCKWORTH, M.A.

Formerly Post Master of Merton College, Oxford ;
Representative in Cyprus of the Eastern Church Association.

CONTENTS.—Catechising, its Importance, Purpose, and Method—The Teaching of the Greek Church on the Bible and Tradition—Free-Will—Original Sin—Redemption—Faith and Works—The Eucharist—Confession and Penance—Invocation of Saints—Icons and Relics—The Intermediate State—The Orthodox Church and Transubstantiation.

Published for the Eastern Church Association.

Crown 8vo. 5s. net.

The Elements of Christian Doctrine

By the REV. T. A. LACEY, M.A., Vicar of Madingley.

CONTENTS.—The Nature of Christian Doctrine—The Content of Christian Doctrine—The Proportion of Faith—Of God and Creation—Concerning Human Life—Concerning Redemption—Concerning the Church—Concerning Practical Religion.

'This is a very able and interesting book, written with the clearness that results from an adequate grasp of the subject and a well defined conception of what the writer aimed at accomplishing.'—**Church Quarterly Review.**

'. . . We must leave our readers to find out for themselves the great help which they may derive in clearing their conceptions, and balancing their beliefs, from this carefully-planned book. It is just the sort of treatise which a man requires who wishes to know, who is not afraid to think, who is desirous to read, but requires some one to guide him.'—**Church Times.**

'Mr. Lacey's book on Christian Doctrine will add to his reputation for theological learning and for close reasoning. It is probably the most ambitious work that he has as yet given to the public, and it is written throughout with the gravity and precision which are appropriate to the great subject with which it deals.—**The Pilot.**

'It will find readers who would never look at a volume of systematic theology, and when it finds them, it will help them to think and give them something to think about.'—**Expository Times.**

'For special commendation we select chap. iv. "Concerning the Church," but the book is excellent throughout, and should become not only a text-book but a standard text-book. It might be added, with advantage to the syllabus of every theological college and read with profit by every layman, and by not a few of the clergy. We cordially commend it.'—**Anglo-Catholic.**

'Those who want a brief guide to correct thinking, which lies at the bottom of wisely energetic life, can hardly do better than make the acquaintance of Mr. Lacey.'—**Church Review.**

'The book is correct, clear, concise, and as far as possible, interesting.'—**Churchman, New York.**

Crown 8vo. 6s. net.

The Minor Festivals
of the Anglican Calendar

By the REV. W. J. SPARROW SIMPSON, M.A.,
Vicar of St. Mark's, Regent's Park.

'This is an excellent book, both in design and execution. . . . A well-written, well-balanced, and thoroughly devout volume. It is eminently readable from beginning to end.'—**Scottish Guardian.**

'With these excellent sketches at their disposal, it is hoped that many more preachers will use the opportunity the Calendar affords for dispelling the blank ignorance of Church history which is one of our English characteristics.'—**Pilot.**

'Of Mr. Simpson's work, it may be said that he has exercised the one quality which is necessary to a book of this character. He has exercised restraint, without which he must have landed his readers on the shores of wild conjecture and unlimited myth. He has also exercised the historical faculty, and at the same time, has recognised possibilities in the spiritual sphere which are impossible to those who have been unable to penetrate beyond purely material conceptions. The book is a real gain to the menological literature of the English Church.'—**Church Times.**

London : 34 King Street, Covent Garden.

In Two Volumes.   Crown 8vo.   6s. each net.   Sold separately.

The Crown of Christ

Spiritual Readings for the Liturgical Year

By the Rev. REGINALD E. HUTTON,
Chaplain of S. Margaret's, East Grinstead.

With a Preface by the Rev. ALFRED G. MORTIMER, D.D.,
Rector of St. Mark's, Philadelphia.

VOL. I.—ADVENT TO EASTER.—Containing Readings for that period, with a course of readings on the 'Seven Words from the Cross,' and readings for the Festivals of the Blessed Virgin Mary during the Advent to Easter Season. *6s. net.*

VOL. II.—EASTER TO ADVENT. *6s. net.*

'We know no recent devotional work quite like the present volume, and we are glad to recommend it specially.'—**Guardian.**

'The meditations are marked with the same freshness of thought as in the previous volume, and the practical application to Christian living is quite excellent.—**Pilot.**

'A devout Churchman living in the world will find it vigorous in thought, beautiful in language, Catholic in sentiment, and, as regards its theology, unexceptionable. . . . Will help to deepen the spiritual lives of Christian men and women, and will be found of no small value to clergymen in suggesting thoughts and subjects for their weekly sermons.—**Church Review.**

'They are full of deep and spiritual thoughts. What adds value to the book is a set of short passages for reading during the week, all bearing upon the Sunday reading. We thoroughly recommend this second volume of Mr. Hutton's spiritual readings. Indeed we consider this book both helpful for the spiritual life, and useful for instruction in the Faith.'—**Church Times.**

'It is in close touch, intellectually and spiritually with the first volume, which we found exceptionally fresh. Together the volumes give us at once a manual of devotion and a manual of theology, and both thoroughly Anglican.'—**Expository Times.**

'He combines vigour of thought with grace of expression that is rather uncommon. We should think the work most useful for its suggestiveness to preachers, though it can be used as a manual of daily devotion.'—**New York Churchman.**

'We cannot praise too highly these two volumes. Mr. Hutton has given us a series of instructions in a style which is both effective and yet free from emotionalism and forced rhetoric. 'The Crown of Christ' is an ideal book for the Catholic layman.—**Indian Church Quarterly Review.**

Demy 8vo. 12s. net.

Synesius the Hellene

By the Rev. W. S. CRAWFORD, B.D.

CONTENTS.—Life of Synesius—The Philosopher—The Man of Science—The Literary Man—The Poet—The Man of Action—The Ecclesiastic—The Humorist—The Country Gentleman—The Man—The Friends of Synesius—The Works of Synesius—Summary—Appendices.

Demy 8vo. 10s.

The Soothsayer Balaam

Or, The Transformation of a Sorcerer into a Prophet.

By the Very Rev. SERAPHIM,
Bishop of Ostrojsk.

CONTENTS.—The Determination of Balak—The Blessing and the Curse—Balaam—The Trial and the Warning—A Blessing instead of a Curse—Balaam's Place in History—The Moral Signification of Balaam's History—Appendix.

Second Edition. Crown 8vo. 6s. net.

Five Great Oxford Leaders
Keble—Newman—Pusey—Liddon—Church

By the Rev. AUG. B. DONALDSON, M.A.,
Canon Residentiary and Precentor of Truro.

'Careful sympathetic character sketches.'—Guardian.

'The merit of the book before us is that it brings each of the five lives into a reasonable compass; sets them, by a careful and constant insistence on dates, in their true relation with one another and with public events: shows with sympathy and without partisanship the special gifts and performances of each man, and leaves on the mind a clear-cut impression of five very different personalities.'—Speaker.

'The author has succeeded in the very difficult task of giving in a short space a clear and accurate presentation, vivid though sober.'—Church Quarterly Review.

Crown 8vo. 2s. net.

Aids to the Devotional Study of the Bible

By the Rev. HERBERT E. HALL, M.A.,
Vicar of St. Peter's, Staines.

With a Preface by the Right Rev. A. F. WINNINGTON INGRAM, D.D.,
Bishop of London.

CONTENTS.—The object and method of the Bible—The chief ways of reading the Bible—The Inspiration of the Bible—Some consequences of the Inspiration of the Bible—Preliminary preparation for the study of our Saviour's life—The purpose and aim of the Four Gospels—The synopsis and plan of the Four Gospels.

London: 34 King Street, Covent Garden.

A 2

Crown 8vo.   3s. 6d.

Happy Suffering (La Bonne Souffrance)

By FRANÇOIS COPPÉE.
Translated by CATHERINE M. WELBY.
With a Preface by W. H. HUTTON, B.D.

'We commend this book to all who care for delicate, graceful writing.'—**Guardian.**

'The little essays which compose the book are most delightful reading.—**Leeds' Mercury.**

'On the beauty and value of suffering to the soul he is never tired of insisting, and this little book may comfort and help many a like sufferer, for whom it would have been a sealed document untranslated.'—**Oxford Magazine.**

Crown 8vo.   1s. 6d.

The Food of Immortality

Instructions on the Sixth Chapter of the Gospel according to St. John.

By the REV. W. B. TREVELYAN, M.A.,
Vicar of St. Matthew's, Westminster.

'This little book of instructions on the sixth chapter of St. John should prove helpful to many: the tone is thoroughly devotional, and the matter catholic. It is suggested that these notes should be made the basis of meditations, and not merely read through and laid aside.'—**Pilot.**

'We can confidently recommend the book both to the clergy and laity.'—**Guardian.**

'We welcome very warmly Mr. Trevelyan's small but most valuable book. . . .'—**Church Times.**

'Reverent in tone, and expressed in beautiful language, it is just such a little book as one would wish to give to the rather better educated of one's Confirmation candidates.'—**Scottish Guardian.**

Crown 16mo.   Cloth limp, 1s. net; cloth boards 1s. 3d. net, or cloth extra gilt edges, 1s. 6d. net.

The Pilgrim's Path

A Book of Prayer for Busy People
With Instructions and Illustrations.

Compiled by FREDERICK E. MORTIMER,
Rector of St. Mark's Church, Jersey City, U.S.A.

With a Preface by the Rev. ALFRED G. MORTIMER, D.D.,
Rector of St. Mark's, Philadelphia.

It is brief, yet supplying all ordinary needs, simple yet most reverent and devotional. Brief as this manual is, it is very comprehensive, providing for almost every exigency of spiritual life. Besides the daily prayers for ordinary needs, provision will be found for occasions of health and sickness, penitence and thanksgiving. In a word, the Christian Pilgrim has here a very valuable guide-book for his path heavenwards.

Thirteen editions of this book have been issued in America,

'Dr. Mortimer says that he has already proved the usefulness of the book in his own parish, and in the United States it has stood the test of four years' circulation, and has passed through thirteen editions. We hope that even a wider sphere will be occupied by the book in the Church of England.'—**Guardian.**

London: 34 King Street, Covent Garden.

Crown 8vo. 3s. 6d.

A Short History of the Church in Great Britain

By WILLIAM HOLDEN HUTTON, B.D.,

Fellow and Tutor of S. John's College, Oxford;
Examining Chaplain to the Lord Bishop of Ely.
Author of ' An Elementary History of the Church in Great Britain.'

This volume is designed to fill a place between Mr. Wakeman's larger volume (see page 18) and the writer's Elementary History (see page 14), both issued by Messrs. Rivington. Mr. Hutton's book differs from Mr. Wakeman's in being somewhat more detailed in its record of events, and including also the History of the Church in Scotland.

'No one is more fitted to write such a book. . . . It is interesting, accurate, and for its size, very full of matter.'—**Literature.**

'Mr. Hutton has written a good book.' —**Spectator.**

'We have been surprised to find how much Mr. Hutton tells in his few pages, and attribute his success to a keen sense for the essential and a terse, yet easy style.'—**Pall Mall Gazette.**

'We have found his book thoroughly readable, and, no doubt, it will be widely read.'—**Speaker.**

'It is a clear and interesting summary of the facts that make up the story of the Anglican Church, which cannot but prove useful to students and teachers of its subject as an introduction to the heavier histories.'—**Scotsman.**

'It is admirable, and, as a text-book on the important subject of which it treats, should prove invaluable.'—**Anglo-Catholic.**

'This is a useful as well as attractive little book. From beginning to end it is careful, accurate, and well thought out.' **Manchester Guardian.**

'The very book for which many have been looking—comprehensive, lucid, and fair.'—**St. James's Gazette.**

'We have seldom come across a more succinct, well-balanced, and impartial survey. Mr. Hutton is an exact and fair-minded scholar, who understands the art of popular exposition, and as an elementary manual for students of Church history his book is valuable. Not the least useful pages are those which present in chronological outline a great array of important landmarks in national affairs which more or less intimately concern the growth of the English Church. Mr. Hutton writes with easy grace, and evident command of every phase of a far-reaching and complicated subject.'—**Standard.**

'To tell the history of the Church in this island from the martyrdom of St. Alban to the accession of Archbishop Temple in 283 pages is no mean achievement. Mr. Hutton has done this, and done it well.'— **Saturday Review.**

'The account of the Reformation is fairly given. . . . The account of the Evangelical school is given with sympathy.'— **Record.**

'Is written with full knowledge, proper proportion, and wise compression.'— **English Historical Review.**

Crown 8vo. 1s.

The English Reformation

With a Preface on the Archbishops' recent decision.

By the REV. W. H. HUTTON, B.D.,
Fellow and Tutor of S. John's College, Oxford.

London : 34 King Street, Covent Garden.

Crown 8vo.

Rivingtons' Handbooks to The Bible and Prayer Book

For the use of Teachers and Students.

With Introduction, Map, Text, Notes, Schemes of Lessons,
and Blackboard Summaries.

General Editor—The REV. BERNARD REYNOLDS, M.A.,

Archbishops' Inspector of Training Colleges ;
Chief Diocesan Inspector of London, and Prebendary of St. Paul's.

The First Volume of the Pentateuch. The Deliverance from Egypt.
Genesis i. to Exodus xii., *with slight omissions* :
By the Rev. H. C. BATTERBURY, B.A., Assistant Diocesan Inspector
of the Diocese of London.   [*Published.*

The Second Volume of the Pentateuch. The Departure from Egypt to
the Death of Moses. Exodus xiii. to the end of Deuteronomy.
By the Rev. H. C. BATTERBURY, B.A.   [*In preparation.*

The Book of Joshua. *With slight omissions.*
By the Rev. G. H. S. WALPOLE, D.D., Principal of Bede College,
Durham. 2s. 6d.   [*Published.*

The Books of Judges and Ruth. By the Rev. G. H. S. WALPOLE, D.D.
2s. 6d.   [*Published.*

The Monarchy. By the Rev. A. R. WHITHAM, M.A., Principal of Culham
College, Abingdon.   [*In November.*

The Captivity: Daniel, Ezra, Nehemiah, and Esther.
By the Rev. G. W. GARROD, M.A., Principal of the Diocesan Training
College, Ripon.   [*In preparation.*

The Gospel According to St. Matthew.
By the Rev. W. C. E. NEWBOLT, M.A., Canon and Chancellor of
St. Paul's. 2s. 6d.   [*Published.*

The Gospel According to St. Mark. By the Rev. F. L. H. MILLARD,
M.A., formerly Diocesan Inspector of Carlisle. 2s. 6d. [*Published.*

The Gospel According to St. Luke.
By the Rev. MORLEY STEVENSON, M.A., Principal of the Training
College, Warrington. 2s. 6d.   [*Just published.*

The Gospel According to St. John.
By the Rev. G. W. DANIELL, M.A., Chaplain of Dulwich College,
Examining Chaplain to the Bishop of Rochester, and Hon. Canon
of Rochester Cathedral.   [*In preparation.*

The Acts of the Apostles. By the Rev. BERNARD REYNOLDS, M.A.
                                                [*In preparation.*

The Prayer Book. By the Rev. BERNARD REYNOLDS, M.A.
                                                [*In preparation.*

London : 34 King Street, Covent Garden.

The object of the series is to help teachers, especially those engaged in primary schools, in their own study for examinations, and in their teaching. The commonest question asked by teachers is, 'What book do you recommend?' These books are a practical answer to that question.

For Pupil-teachers and students in Training Colleges, such information will be gathered together as those who have been conversant with the work for a long time have found to be most necessary and helpful.

A prominent feature of the books is the schemes for Lessons, which it is hoped will guide teachers in impressing upon the minds of the young the spiritual, doctrinal, and practical points which it is their object to impress. A great difficulty of teachers, even of those who know their subjects well, is to see exactly the points that will be of use to learners, points to be impressed, not only upon their minds, but upon their lives.

For those who want to go more deeply into matters, there are Additional Notes upon matters that the teacher should know but need not teach : for the teacher must know a great deal more than he teaches.

A new series of mere commentaries is not wanted, considering the many excellent works that already exist, but there are few books at present which look at the subject from the teacher's point of view. These volumes are designed to help both to teach and to learn, but especially the former.

In Rivingtons' Bible Handbooks the correct translation of the text will be carefully attended to ; in the Prayer Book, the lessons taught by the history of Christian religion and thought will be dwelt upon.

The chief causes of separation from the Church are misunderstanding of the Bible and ignorance of history ; these books are written with the object of helping teachers to overcome these difficulties.

Crown 8vo.

Text Books on the Prayer Book

For the use of Candidates at the Oxford and Cambridge local Examinations, and others. By the Rev. SEPTIMUS BUSS, LL.B., Rector of St. Anne and St. Agnes, Gresham Street.

The Morning and Evening Prayer and the Litany. 1s.
The Offices for Holy Communion, Baptism, and Confirmation. 1s.
The Church Catechism. 1s. 4d.   **The Three Creeds.** 1s. 6d.

'Thank you very much for your useful little book. It ought to be of great value for an intelligent teaching of the Prayer Book.'—**The Right Rev. Bishop Creighton.**

'Many thanks for sending me a copy of your excellent book, which I think well calculated for its object.'—**Archdeacon Sinclair.**

'The book is one we can thoroughly recommend to the ordinary reader from first to last, its arrangement is such that the student finds his points ready to hand, and interestingly set out.'—**School Guardian.**

'From beginning to end the manual is excellent. . . . It needs only to be known to command a considerable sale. It deals fairly and straightly with the three offices.'—**School Guardian.**

'All the important dates and facts are mentioned. A knowledge of all that is so clearly set forth by the author would greatly aid the proper understanding and appreciation of the Prayer Book.'—**Church Review.**

'An excellent introduction to the critical study of the Prayer Book. Mr. Buss keeps the historical value of the English Liturgy well in view.'—**Educational Times.**

London : 34 King Street, Covent Garden.

Small Fcap. 8vo.   1s. each net.

Oxford Church Text Books

General Editor—The REV. LEIGHTON PULLAN, M.A.,
Fellow of S. John's College, and Lecturer in Theology
at S. John's, Oriel, and Queen's Colleges, Oxford.

A Comprehensive Series of Cheap and Scholarly Manuals dealing with the more important branches of Religious Knowledge.

It is felt that there is a decided need for such manuals for the use of students of Theology, candidates for Ordination, higher classes in Schools, and for Church Guilds. The Manuals are written in full sympathy with definite Anglican doctrine, and thus, it is hoped, will meet a widely-felt and expressed want.

The Series includes books on Biblical, Doctrinal, Liturgical, and Historical subjects. Attention is devoted to Scottish ecclesiastical history, as well as English, so that members both of the Church of England and of the Episcopal Church of Scotland are provided with manuals written in accordance with their own convictions.

The Hebrew Prophets.
The Rev. R. L. OTTLEY, M.A., Rector of Winterbourne Bassett; formerly Principal of Pusey House, Oxford.   [*Published.*

Outlines of Old Testament Theology.
The Rev. C. F. BURNEY, M.A., Lecturer in Hebrew at and Librarian of St. John's College, Oxford.   [*Published.*

The Text of the New Testament.
The Rev. K. LAKE, M.A., Curate of S. Mary the Virgin's, Oxford.
          [*Published.*

Early Christian Doctrine.
The Rev. LEIGHTON PULLAN, M.A.   [*Published.*

An Elementary History of the Church in Great Britain.
The Rev. W. H. HUTTON, B.D., Fellow and Tutor of St. John's College, Oxford, Examining Chaplain to the Bishop of Ely.   [*Published.*
Recommended by the Lecturers of the Church Committee for Church Defence.

The Reformation in Great Britain.
H. O. WAKEMAN, M.A., Late Fellow of All Souls' College, Oxford, and the Rev. LEIGHTON PULLAN, M.A.   [*Published.*

The History of the Book of Common Prayer.
The Rev. J. H. MAUDE, M.A., Examining Chaplain to the Bishop of St. Albans   [*Published.*

London: 34 King Street, Covent Garden.

The Articles of the Church of England. In Two Volumes.
Vol. I.—History and Explanation of Articles i.-viii. } *May also be had*
Vol. II.—Explanation of Articles ix.-xxxix. } *in one vol.* 2s.
The Rev. B. J. KIDD, B.D., Keble College, Oxford. *[Published.*

A Manual for Confirmation.
The Rev. T. FIELD, D.D., Warden of Radley College. *[Published.*

Church History to A.D. 325.
The Rev. II. N. BATE, M.A., Examining Chaplain to the Bishop of London. *[Published.*

The Reformation on the Continent.
The Rev. B. J. KIDD, B.D., Keble College, Tutor of Non-Collegiate Students, Oxford. *[In the press.*

Old Testament History. In two volumes.
The Rev. T. F. HOBSON, M.A., Head Master of the King's School, Rochester. *[In preparation.*

An Introduction to the New Testament.
The Rev. LEIGHTON PULLAN, M.A. *[In preparation.*

The Teaching of St. Paul.
The Rev. E. W. M. O. DE LA HEY, M.A., Tutor of Keble College, Oxford. *[In preparation.*

Evidences of Christianity.
The Rev. L. RAGG, M.A., Warden of the Bishop's Hostel, Lincoln. *[In preparation.*

The Apostles' Creed.
The Rev. H. F. D. MACKAY, M.A., Merton College, and Pusey House, Oxford. *[In preparation.*

The Church, its Ministry and Authority.
The Rev. DARWELL STONE, M.A., Principal of the Missionary College, Dorchester. *[In preparation.*

Mediæval Church Missions.
C. R. BEAZLEY, M.A., Fellow of Merton College, Oxford. *[In preparation.*

A History of the Church in the United States of America.
The Right Rev. LEIGHTON COLEMAN, D.D., LL.D., Bishop of Delaware, U.S.A. *[In preparation.*

A Comparative History of Religions.
The Rev. LEIGHTON PULLAN, M.A. *[In preparation.*

A History of the Rites of the Church.
The Rev. F. E. BRIGHTMAN, M.A., Pusey House, Oxford. *[In preparation.*

Instructions in Christian Doctrine.
The Rev. V. S. S. COLES, M.A., Principal of Pusey House, Oxford. *[In preparation.*

The Future State.
The Rev. S. C. GAYFORD, M.A., Vice-Principal of Cuddesdon College *[In preparation*

London : 34 King Street, Covent Garden.

Crown 8vo. 1s. 6d. each.

Rivingtons' Edition of the Books of the Bible

With Introduction, Notes, Maps, and Plans.

General Editor—The REV. A. E. HILLARD, M.A.,
Head Master of Durham School.

The Book of Genesis. By the Rev. T. C. FRY, D.D.,
Headmaster of Berkhamsted School.   [*Published.*

The Book of Exodus. By the Rev. H. F. STEWART, M.A.,
Chaplain of Trinity College, Cambridge.   [*Just ready.*

The Book of Joshua. By the Rev. F. W. SPURLING, M.A.,
Vice-Principal of Keble College, Oxford.   [*Published.*

The Book of Judges. By the Rev. H. F. STEWART, M.A. [*Published.*

The Book of Ruth and the First Book of Samuel. In One Vol.
By the Rev. P. W. H. KETTLEWELL, M.A., Assistant Master at
Clifton College.   [*Published.*

The Second Book of Samuel. By the Rev. LONSDALE RAGG, M.A.,
Warden of the Bishop's Hostel, Lincoln.   [*Published.*

The First Book of Kings. By the Rev. W. O. BURROWS, M.A.,
Vicar of Holy Trinity, Leeds.   [*Published.*

The Second Book of Kings. By the Rev. W. O. BURROWS, M.A.
[*Published.*

The Books of Ezra and Nehemiah. In One Volume.
By the Rev. P. W. H. KETTLEWELL, M.A.

The Book of Amos. By the Rev. W. O. BURROWS, M.A.

St. Matthew's Gospel. By the Rev. A. E. HILLARD, M.A. } *Published.*

St. Mark's Gospel. By the Rev. A. E. HILLARD, M.A.

St. Luke's Gospel. By the Rev. A. E. HILLARD, M.A.

St. John's Gospel. By the Rev. A. E. HILLARD, M.A.

'The introductions are sober, scholarly, and well written, containing just the kind of help and information that is needed by young students. The notes are at once luminous and concise, never obtrusive or superfluous, and yet full of illustrations from other parts of the Bible. . . . We cannot but think that many of the less learned candidates for Holy Orders would produce better Bible work than they at present do if they had recourse to books of this truly expository character, instead of to others published at a larger price, and furnished with a larger amount of "padding."'—**Guardian.**

'The text is well edited on the lines which have made these "Books of the Bible" so widely used in England' (The Second Book of Kings).—**Scotsman.**

'Mr. Burrows supplies a great deal of useful information, and his interpretations of the text are often luminous'(The Second Book of Kings).—**Educational Times.**

'Will be a valuable help both to teachers and older scholars. There are already eight other volumes, and by buying these and each new volume as it appears, managers will provide their schools with a valuable Bible commentary at a very small price' (The Second Book of Samuel).—**School Guardian.**

'This is a very good piece of work' (The First Book of Kings).—**Spectator.**

London: 34 King Street, Covent Garden.

In Eight Volumes. Crown 8vo. 6s. net each.
The Complete Set £2, 8s. net.

Periods of European History

General Editor—ARTHUR HASSALL, M.A.,
Student of Christ Church, Oxford.

THE object of this series is to present in separate Volumes a comprehensive and trustworthy account of the general development of European History, and to deal fully and carefully with the more prominent events in each century.

No such attempt to place the History of Europe in a comprehensive, detailed, and readable form before the English Public has previously been made, and the Series forms a valuable continuous History of Mediæval and Modern Europe.

Period I.—The Dark Ages. 476-918.

By C. W. C. OMAN, M.A., Deputy Chichele Professor of Modern History in the University of Oxford. *6s. net.*

Period II.—The Empire and the Papacy. 918-1273.

By T. F. TOUT, M.A., Professor of History at the Owens College, Victoria University, Manchester. *6s. net.*

Period III.—The Close of the Middle Ages. 1273-1494.

By R. LODGE, M.A., Professor of History at the University of Edinburgh. *6s. net.*

Period IV.—Europe in the 16th Century. 1494-1598.

By A. H. JOHNSON, M.A., Historial Lecturer to Merton, Trinity, and University Colleges, Oxford. *6s. net.*

Period V.—The Ascendancy of France. 1598-1715.

By H. O. WAKEMAN, M.A., late Fellow of All Souls' College, Oxford. *6s. net.*

Period VI.—The Balance of Power. 1715-1789.

By A. HASSALL, M.A. *6s. net.*

Period VII.—Revolutionary Europe. 1789-1815.

By H. MORSE STEPHENS, M.A., Professor of History at Cornell University, Ithaca, U.S.A. *6s. net.*

Period VIII.—Modern Europe. 1815-1899.

By W. ALISON PHILLIPS, M.A., formerly Senior Scholar of St. John's College, Oxford. *6s. net.*

London: 34 King Street, Covent Garden.

Sixth Edition. Crown 8vo. 7s. 6d.

An Introduction to the History of the Church of England

From the Earliest Times to the Present Day.

By H. O. WAKEMAN, M.A.,

Late Fellow of All Souls' College, Oxford,
Author of ' The Ascendancy of France '
(Periods of European History).

' The most precious history of the Church of England that has ever been written, a book scholarlike, lucid, full of matter, full of interest, just and true, and inspired with faith, hope and charity, as few Church histories, or any other histories, have ever been.'—**The Right Rev. Bishop Stubbs.**

' Mr. Wakeman's book is not only scholarly and thoughtful, but is also written so easily and clearly that it will be read with interest by the large class of general readers who are interested in its subject. It is the first book which has succeeded in presenting the history of the Church of England in a clear and intelligible form.'—
The Right Rev. Bishop Creighton.

' Will at once and satisfactorily fill up a long-felt void.'—**The late Rev. Canon Bright, Christ Church, Oxford.**

' Mr. Wakeman's "History of the English Church" was the book that we wanted. No Churchman of average education has now any excuse for ignorance of the history of his Church; nor any schoolmaster or mistress for omitting to teach it to their boys and girls.'—
The Rev. Canon Gore, Westminster.

' It is just what was wanted. . . .' —
The Rev. H. L. Thompson, Vicar of St. Mary's, Oxford.

' I fully recognise the value of Mr. Wakeman's work.'—**The Bishop of Lichfield.**

' I find it a fascinating book, marked by fairness of mind and a just sense of proportion.'—**The Rev. W. O. Burrows, formerly Principal of the Clergy School, Leeds.**

' I shall be happy to recommend it to my classes. . . . I cannot speak too highly of this work.'—**The Rev. E. Elmer Harding, Principal of Lichfield Theological College.**

' I think Mr. Wakeman's work is excellently done, and I am quite sure the book will be found most useful by theological students. I shall mention it wherever I can.'—**The Rev. Dr. Maclear, Warden of S. Augustine's College, Canterbury.**

' Will have much pleasure in making it known.'—**The Rev. Canon Worlledge, Truro.**

' I have recommended it as a text-book to the students of this college.'—
The Rev. J. S. Teulon, Principal of the Theological College, Chichester.

' It does not often fall to the reviewer's lot to be able to give such unreserved praise as can be given to this most charming book.'—**Guardian.**

' Will succeed not only in satisfying a great and admitted want, but will also occupy a foremost place as an accredited text-book.'—**Church Times.**

' The debt Churchmen owe to this splendid little volume can hardly be exaggerated.'—**Church Review.**

Second Edition, revised. Crown 8vo. 2s. 6d.

Why we are Churchmen

Seven Plain Reasons.

By A. L. OLDHAM, M.A., Prebendary of Hereford,

Rector of St. Leonard's, Bridgnorth, and Rural Dean.

With a Preface by EDGAR C. S. GIBSON, M.A.,
Vicar of Leeds.

London : 34 King Street, Covent Garden.

Crown 8vo. 3s. 6d. net.

In Memoriam Crucis

The Daily Sequence of The Holy Week

Written and Compiled by

· GEORGE DEVEREUX DAVENPORT, M.A.,

Vicar of Kewstoke.

With an Introduction by GEORGE BODY, D.D.,

Canon Missioner of Durham.

'We heartily commend this little book to the clergy, and to devout lay people, in the hope that it may prove of real service in deepening spiritual life.'—

The Church Quarterly Review.

'This thoughtful and earnest volume should prove helpful to many.'—

Church Bells.

'The short Addresses on the Seven Words are suggestive, and have a solemnity not always found in such Addresses.'—

The Church Times.

'The book is divided into six parts. We find in it a happy gift—almost a genius—of selection, style, and arrangements, which gives it a distinct value. The book is admirably produced by Messrs. Rivington.'

—**The Church Review.**

16mo, 1s. net, or in limp lambskin, 1s. 9d. net.

Prayers at the Eucharist
in the words of Holy Scripture

Compiled by SISTERS OF THE COMMUNITY OF S. PETER.

With an Introduction by the Rev. W. H. CLEAVER, M.A.,

Warden of the Community.

The book is an effort to utilise *inspired* words in devotions before, at, and after Holy Communion.

The shape given to these devotions is, for the most part, that of a series of colloquies between the Divine Master and the soul.

'We are glad to commend it.'—**Pilot.**

'The work has been done reverently and

wisely, and should prove helpful to many.

—**Guardian.**

Crown 8vo. 6s. net; or Cheap Edition, 3s. 6d. net.

Present Endurance

Encouraging Words for Life's Journey

A Volume of Readings and Meditations

By ELEANOR TEE,

Author of the 'Sanctuary of Suffering.'

With a Preface by the Rev. W. B. TREVELYAN, M.A.,

Vicar of S. Matthew's, Westminster.

Crown 8vo. 6d. net.

Religious Education in the Home

Hints for the use of Parents of the Upper and Middle Classes.

With a Preface by The Right Rev. GEORGE FORREST BROWNE, D.C.L.,

Lord Bishop of Bristol.

London : 34 King Street, Covent Garden.

With Illustrations. Crown 8vo. 6s. net.

Some Principles and Services of the Prayer Book historically considered

Edited by J. WICKHAM LEGG, F.R.C.P., F.S.A.

CONTENTS.

The Ceremonial Use of Lights in the Second Year of the Reign of King Edward the Sixth. By CUTHBERT ATCHLEY.

The English Altar and Its Surroundings. By J. COMPER.

The Act of 1872 and its Shortened, Hurried, and Extra-Liturgical Services. By J. WICKHAM LEGG.

The Regalism of the Prayer-Book. By J. WICKHAM LEGG.

Demy 8vo. 1s. net.

The Acts of Uniformity

Their Scope and Effect

By the REV. T. A. LACEY, M.A., Vicar of Madingley.

Demy 8vo. 1s. net.

Reservation

A Letter to His Grace the Lord Archbishop of Canterbury.
By the REV. T. A. LACEY, M.A.

Crown 8vo. 2s.

God and Prayer

By the RIGHT REV. BOYD VINCENT, D.D.,
Bishop-Coadjutor of Southern Ohio, U.S.A.

CONTENTS.—Introduction, dealing with the Difficulties connected with Prayer—How can God hear Prayer?—How can God answer Prayer?—Prayers, Why not Answered?

'We thank him for one of the very ablest books we have ever read on the subject of prayer.'—*Guardian.*

Crown 8vo. 3s.

The King's Highway of the Holy Cross— Outlines for Meditations

With a Preface by the VERY REV. H. B. BROMBY,
Vicar of All Saints', Clifton ; sometime Dean of Hobart, Tasmania.

London : 34 King Street, Covent Garden.

Third Edition. Crown 8vo. 1s. 6d.

Some Titles and Aspects of the Eucharist

By the RIGHT REV. E. S. TALBOT, D.D.,

Lord Bishop of Rochester.

'The work deserves a wide circulation.'—*Church Bells.*
'Models of teaching.'—*Church Times.*

Crown 8vo. 5s.

Sermons Preached in the Parish Church of Leeds 1889-1895

By the RIGHT REV. E. S. TALBOT, D.D.,

Lord Bishop of Rochester.

Third Edition. Crown 8vo. 2s. 6d.

A Continuous Narrative of the Life of Christ

In the Words of the Four Gospels.

With Maps, Introduction, and Notes, arranged by

The REV. A. E. HILLARD, M.A.,

Head Master of Durham School.

'It should serve its purpose admirably. . . . The whole work is done in a scholarly fashion, and has the farther merit of being moderate both in size and price. Teachers and others will probably find it more helpful than many elaborate commentaries.'—*Glasgow Herald.*

Second Edition. 16mo. 2s. 6d.

The Christian's Manual

Containing the chief things which a Christian ought to Know, Believe, and Do to his Soul's Health.

By the REV. W. H. H. JERVOIS, M.A.,

Vicar of St. Mary Magdalene's, Munster Square.

With a Preface by the Right Rev. C. C. GRAFTON

Bishop of Fond-du-Lac.

'Without hesitation we recommend this as a valuable gift-book to lads about to be confirmed ; they will not readily forsake it for any other guide to holy living. The get-up of the book is excellent.'—*Church Times.*

'This is the most complete book of the kind that has been published. . . . There is also a specially excellent instruction on Bible reading, which, when done on Mr. Jervois's method, offers a substitute for formal meditation which is likely to be useful to a great number of people. The private prayers for morning and evening supply the very best short form we have met with.'—*Guardian.*

London : 34 King Street, Covent Garden.

Second Edition. Crown 8vo. 7s. 6d.

The Egypt of the Hebrews and Herodotos

By the REV. A. H. SAYCE,

Professor of Assyriology at Oxford.

'On the whole, we know of no more useful handbook to Egyptian history, summing up in a popular form in a short compass the results of Egyptian research down to the present time.'—**Church Times.**

'Professor Sayce has written a charming work, which every lover of Egypt will fly to.'—**Church Bells.**

'Professor Sayce has a story of singular fascination to tell.'—**Yorkshire Post.**

Crown 8vo. 8s. 6d.

The Early History of the Hebrews

By the REV. A. H. SAYCE,

Professor of Assyriology at Oxford ;
Author of 'The Egypt of the Hebrews and Herodotos.'

A fascinating book.'—**Standard.**

'Is charged with mental stimulus on every page.'—**Expository Times.**

'Every page of the book reveals the scholar, and the fascinating manner in which Professor Sayce marshals his facts

and draws his conclusions makes the book of great value to students.'—**Western Morning News.**

'This extremely interesting volume.'—**Church Bells.**

Crown 8vo. 7s. 6d.

The Fire upon the Altar

Sermons preached to Harrow boys. 1887 to 1890.

By the RIGHT REV. J. E. C. WELLDON, D.D.,
Bishop of Calcutta, and Metropolitan of India.

Fcap. 8vo. 1s. 6d.

Clariora Cariora

Or, Lights and Shades of Greek Texts, with Prayers.

By the REV. CANON H. PERCY SMITH, M.A.,
Late Chaplain of Christ Church, Cannes.

Crown 8vo. 5s.

The Power of an Endless Life

And other Sermons.

By DAVID WRIGHT, M.A.,
Late Vicar of Stoke Bishop, Bristol.

With a Preface by the Rev. Canon AINGER, M.A., LL.D.,
Master of the Temple.

London : 34 King Street, Covent Garden.

Fcap. 8vo.   2s.

Considerations for Advent
on the Relation of the Word to the World

By the REV. E. HERMITAGE DAY, M.A.,
Vicar of Abbey Cwmhir, Radnorshire.

Royal 32mo, 2s. 6d., or in limp lambskin, 3s. 6d.
Printed in Red and Black on Toned Paper.

The Little Book of Death and Rest Eternal

Containing the Office of the Dead, with the Commendation of Souls,
according to the Sarum Breviary, Manchester al Mondo, or a Contemplation
of Death and Immortality, and the Contakion for the Departed, as sung in
St. George's Chapel, Windsor, at the Funeral of the late Queen.

Second Edition.   Royal 32mo.   One Vol.   2s.
Or in 2 vols. (the 'Hours' and 'Mirror' separately).   2s. 6d.
[Copies may also be had in sheets, complete.   1s. 6d.]

The Hours of the Blessed Virgin Mary

According to the Sarum Breviary, together with
a brief Commentary from 'The Mirror of our Lady.'

Royal Quarto.   £2, 2s. net, in sheets only.

An Altar Book

Containing the Order for the Administration of the Holy Communion,
according to the Book of Common Prayer, together with additional matter
translated from the English Missals of the earlier part of the Sixteenth
Century.   Edited by A COMMITTEE OF PRIESTS.

Small Fcap. 8vo.   3s. 6d.
May also be had bound in leather.

Daily Footsteps in the Church's Path

Being Daily Readings in Prose and Verse
arranged in the Order of the Church's Year.
Compiled by E. L. B. C., and M. B.
With a Preface by the Rev. THOMAS B. DOVER, M.A.,
Vicar of Old Malden, Surrey.

'This is an excellent example of its class, and contains some features not commonly found in similar books.'—Guardian.

'The selections are wisely chosen from a wide and varied set of writers, and afford good and wholesome food for daily thought.'—Church Bells.

'An attractive manual of devotional reading, which will be all the more welcome to many because it is introduced by a preface from the pen of the Rev. Thomas B. Dover.'—Scotsman.

London: 34 King Street, Covent Garden.

Crown 8vo. 4s. 6d.

The Mystery of the Cross

Being Eight Addresses on the Atonement

By the REV. W. O. BURROWS, M.A.,

Vicar of Holy Trinity, Leeds.

Such sermons as the eight in this volume are rare indeed. . . . The whole volume deserves, and will repay, close study, and priest or layman who masters it will find his theology enriched and his devotion quickened by it.'—**Church Times.**

Third Edition. Crown 8vo. 3s. 6d.

From Advent to Advent

Sermons preached at the Chapel Royal, Whitehall.
By the late AUBREY L. MOORE, M.A.
With a Preface by the Rev. WALTER LOCK, D.D.,
Warden of Keble College, Oxford.

Second Impression. Crown 8vo. 3s. 6d.

The Message of the Gospel

Addresses to Candidates for Ordination,
and Sermons preached chiefly before the University of Oxford.
By the late AUBREY L. MOORE, M.A.

Fourth Edition. Crown 8vo. 3s. 6d.

Some Aspects of Sin

Three Courses of Sermons.
By the late AUBREY L. MOORE, M.A.

Second Edition. Crown 8vo. 1s. net.

The Prayer Book

Notes and Questions intended to help towards its teaching
in Middle Forms of Public Schools.

By E. C. WICKHAM, D.D.,
Dean of Lincoln.

Third Edition. Crown 8vo. 1s. net.

The Church Catechism

Notes and Questions intended to help towards its teaching
in Middle Forms of Public Schools.

By E. C. WICKHAM, D.D.,
Dean of Lincoln.

London: 34 King Street, Covent Garden.

Crown 8vo. 2s. 6d. net.

Christianity and Paganism
in the Fourth and Fifth Centuries

By ERNEST N. BENNETT, M.A.,
Fellow and Lecturer of Hertford College, Oxford.

CONTENTS.—Causes which retarded the overthrow of Paganism—Methods of direct Coercion employed against Paganism—The inherent weakness of Paganism—The fitness of Christianity to take its place—The last days of Paganism.

'The historians and even the original documents have been studied and sifted. It is brief but authoritative.'—**Expository Times.**

'We feel we can confidently recommend this little work to candidates for University and other examinations (as Cambridge Theological Preliminary for Holy Orders) whose course does not stop short at the Council of Chalcedon.'—**University Correspondent.**

'He has stated clearly and forcibly the various forms taken by the attack on the ancient religion, and, what is more important, its inability to resist the attack owing to the lack of cohesion, and failure to satisfy the religious needs of the world.'—**Oxford Magazine.**

Demy 8vo. 25s.

Holy Matrimony

A Treatise on the Divine Laws of Marriage.

By OSCAR D. WATKINS, M.A.,
Archdeacon of Lucknow.

CONTENTS.—The Divine Institution of Marriage—The Three Characters of Marriage as found in History—Marriage in the State of Innocence—The Fall and the Corruption of all Flesh—Marriage after the Fall and outside Christianity—Christian or Holy Matrimony—The Indissolubility of Christian Marriage: and Divorce—The Re-Marriage of Converts and Mixed Marriages—Polygamy—The Marriage of Near Kin—Index.

Small Fcap. 8vo. 1s.
May also be had bound in leather.

The Way of Happiness

Or, The Art of being Happy and making others so.
Translated and Adapted from the French
By CATHERINE M. WELBY.
With a Preface by W. H. HUTTON, B.D.

London: 34 King Street, Covent Garden.

Crown 8vo. 6s. net.

How to Prepare Essays, Lectures, Articles, Books, Speeches, and Letters

With Hints on writing for the Press

By EUSTACE H. MILES, M.A.

Formerly Scholar of King's College, Cambridge.

'A manual very well done.'—**Manchester Guardian.**

'It is crammed with useful hints.'—**Oxford Magazine.**

'Mr. Miles' experience as an Honours Coach in Essay-writing at Cambridge University has enabled him to supply this useful book on a vague and difficult class

of subjects, such as the expression of ideas, style, speaking, proof-correcting. . . The work teems with useful suggestions not only for pupils, but also for teachers and examiners.'—**Educational Times.**

'Will certainly help a student in mastering the mechanical processes of literary work.'—**Aberdeen Journal.**

Crown 8vo. 3s.

Souvenirs of Cranford

And other Sketches

By BEATRIX L. TOLLEMACHE.

(Hon. Mrs. Lionel Tollemache).

CONTENTS. — Cranford Souvenirs—Should Auld Acquaintance be Forgot—The Naval Chaplain—Sunset—An Alpine Quarterdeck—Charles Victor de Bonstetten—A Glimpse of Mediæval Life—The Childhood of Georges Sand—A Fable on Home Rule—A Fable : The Chimney-pot—A Fable on Censoriousness—The Trees of the Forest—An Eighteenth-Century Ruskin.

'Will be read with delight by all the cult of Mrs. Gaskell.'—**Scotsman.**

'This is a charming collection of essays and sketches, which says much for the writer's culture and taste, and especially

for her intimate acquaintance with some neglected by-paths of literature, both British and French. . . . Altogether, this book is very delightful reading.'—**Glasgow Herald.**

Quarto. 5s.

The Idylls of Theocritus

Translated into English Verse.

By JAMES HENRY HALLARD, M.A., Oxon.

'This faithful, scholarly, and tasteful book brings within reach of the English reader a poet who, in our opinion, ought to hold a place among the very foremost of those unapproachable singers whom ancient Hellas brought forth—the poet who could bring into the dusty streets of

Alexandria airs that—

Smelt rich of lush summer and autumn boon,

whose genius (in the eloquent words of Mr. Andrew Lang) "leaped like a many-coloured flame from the embers on an extinguished altar." '—**Pilot.**

London : 34 King Street, Covent Garden.

*Post Free to Subscribers, Ten Shillings a year, paid in advance;
or Three Shillings a Number.*

The Economic Review

CONTENTS OF THE OCTOBER NUMBER, 1901.

Brooke Foss Westcott. Rev. T. C. FRY.

Profit-Sharing—A Vindication. GEORGE LIVESEY.

Effects of Colonization in British Guiana. HENRY KIRKE.

The Philosophy of the Workmen's Hotel Movement.
JOHN GARRETT LEIGH.

Progress and Deterioration in the Co-operative Movement.
HENRY W. WOLFF.

The Housing of a Provincial City. Rev. A. J. CARLYLE.

Legislation, Parliamentary Inquiries and Official Returns.
EDWIN CANNAN, M.A.

Notes and Memoranda.—Reviews and Short Notices.

Crown 8vo. 2s.

The New Trades Combination Movement

Its Principles, Methods, and Progress.

By E. J. SMITH.

With an Introduction by the Rev. J. CARTER, M.A.,
Bursar of Pusey House, Oxford.

Demy 8vo. 16s.

A History of the Theories of Production and Distribution in English Political Economy, from 1776 to 1848

By EDWIN CANNAN, M.A., Balliol College, Oxford.

Crown 8vo. 1s. 6d.

The London Diocese Book

Church Calendar and General Almanack for 1901.

Issued under the sanction of the LORD BISHOP OF LONDON.

London : 34 King Street, Covent Garden.

Third Edition, revised. In Two Volumes. Crown 8vo. 16s.
With numerous Illustrations.

Old Touraine
The Life and History of the Famous Châteaux of France.
By THEODORE ANDREA COOK, B.A.,
Sometime Scholar of Wadham College, Oxford.

'It was a happy inspiration which induced Mr. T. A. Cook to devote a monograph to this subject. . . . The conception is at once felicitous and novel, no similar work having been produced either in England or in France, and the execution is worthy of the conception.'—**Times.**

Second Edition. Demy 8vo. With Maps. 16s.

Venice
An Historical Sketch of the Republic
By HORATIO F. BROWN,
Author of 'Life on the Lagoons.'

'Venice holds so high a place in the affections of all who are sensible to the charms of beauty and dignity that Mr. Horatio Brown's excellent sketch of its history is sure to receive a warm welcome. His book has many merits. . . . While giving due prominence to the constitutional history of Venice, he is never dull, and has, indeed, rendered this side of his subject specially interesting.'—**Saturday Review.**

'Mr. Brown has brought to his task both knowledge and sympathy, and the result of his labour is that he has produced a book worthy of his subject. . . . From first to last the story is one of absorbing interest.'—**Aberdeen Journal.**

Third Edition. With Illustrations. Crown 8vo. 6s.

Life on the Lagoons
By HORATIO F. BROWN,
Author of 'Venice: An Historical Sketch.'

'No writer since Mr. Ruskin has so thoroughly entered into the charm of Venice as Mr. Horatio Brown, and to this he adds an intimate knowledge of her history. In the new edition of "Life on the Lagoons" he has rewritten the chapter on the structure of the Venetian Estuary, and added a brief but not insufficient history of the city. In its new and illustrated form it will even better than before serve as an excellent guide-book to those who are happy enough to be in Venice, and a constant recall to those who would fain be there again.'—**Guardian.**

Crown 8vo. 6s.

Art and Life and the Building
and Decoration of Cities
Arts and Crafts Lectures.
By T. J. COBDEN SANDERSON; W. R. LETHABY;
WALTER CRANE; REGINALD BLOMFIELD; HALSEY RICARDO,
Members of the Arts and Crafts Exhibition Society.

London : 34 King Street, Covent Garden.

Small Fcap. 8vo. 3s. 6d.
May also be had bound in leather.

Words and Days

A Table Book of Prose and Verse.

Compiled by BOWYER NICHOLS.

With a Preface by GEORGE SAINTSBURY.

Professor of Rhetoric and English Literature
in the University of Edinburgh.

'We can only commend the little volume as, in its kind, a nearly faultless production.'—**Times.**

'The selection bears witness to wide reading and refined taste.'—**Westminster Gazette.**

'This is a delightful little book in every respect. Mr. Nichols has performed his difficult task with admirable judgment and excellent taste.'—**Glasgow Herald.**

'Altogether this little book is admirable, and will take its stand among centos as the "Golden Treasury" did among lyrical collections. It is indeed a year's companion, and then will be a friend to live with for many another year.'—**Manchester Guardian.**

'The field covered by the selections is a very wide one, but there is nothing trivial here.'—**Yorkshire Post.**

Second Edition. Demy 16mo. 2s. 6d. net.
May also be had bound in leather.

Seventeenth Century Lyrics

Edited by GEORGE SAINTSBURY.

'Charming in its appearance, and thoroughly delightful in its contents.'—**Times.**

New Edition. Demy 16mo. 2s. 6d.
May also be had bound in leather.

A Calendar of Verse

Being a Short Selection for every day in the year from Twelve Poets, one for each month.

With an Introduction by GEORGE SAINTSBURY.

CONTENTS.—Shakespeare—Spenser—S. T. Coleridge—Herrick—Shelley—William Morris—Keats—Byron—Campion—Sir Walter Scott—Wordsworth—Milton.

'An admirable little book; perhaps the best of its kind in existence.'—**Glasgow Herald.**

'The selections have been well made, and any who wish to store the mind day by day with high thoughts nobly expressed will find the book very much to their liking.'—**Yorkshire Post.**

'Delightful to handle and to look at, delightful to read in.'—**Speaker.**

'The dainty volume will be found a pleasant enough companion. It is prettily got up, and the inevitable introduction is from the graceful pen of Mr. George Saintsbury.'—**Manchester Examiner.**

London: 34 King Street, Covent Garden.

Third Edition. Crown 8vo. 6s. net.

Essays in English Literature

1780 to 1860.

By GEORGE SAINTSBURY,

Professor of Rhetoric and English Literature
in the University of Edinburgh.

Second Edition. Crown 8vo. 6s. net.

Essays on French Novelists

By GEORGE SAINTSBURY.

Second Edition. Crown 8vo. 6s. net.

Miscellaneous Essays

By GEORGE SAINTSBURY.

CONTENTS.—English Prose Style—Chamfort and Rivarol—Modern English Prose (1876)—Ernest Renan—Thoughts on Republics—Saint-Evremond—Charles Baudelaire—The Young England Movement; its place in our History—A Paradox on Quinet—The Contrasts of English and French Literature—A Frame of Miniatures :—Parny, Dorat, Désaugiers, Vadé, Piron, Panard—The Present State of the English Novel (1892).

Second Edition. Crown 8vo. 6s.

Names and their Histories

Alphabetically Arranged as a Handbook of Historical Geography and Topographical Nomenclature.

With Appendices on Indian, Turkish, Slavonic and German Nomenclature, and on Magyar, French Village, and English Village Names.

By ISAAC TAYLOR, M.A., Litt. D., Hon. LL.D.
Canon of York.

Fourteenth Thousand. Fcap. 8vo. 1s. 6d.

Popular Lessons on Cookery

By MRS. BOYD CARPENTER.

London : 34 King Street, Covent Garden.

MESSRS. RIVINGTON *issue the undermentioned Catalogues,
which may be had on application:—*

Demy 8vo.

1. COMPLETE CATALOGUE OF ALL THEIR PUBLICATIONS.

Crown 8vo.

2. A SELECTION FROM RECENT PUBLICATIONS.

Crown 8vo.

3. A CATALOGUE OF EDUCATIONAL WORKS.

Crown 8vo.

4. A LIST OF MEDICAL WORKS.

LONDON: RIVINGTONS

* 9 7 8 3 7 4 3 3 8 4 1 1 8 *